Christmas 1998

To,

Sister L

With

G000153601

xxx xxx xxx xxx

ST ANTHONY OF PADUA

SHEILAH WARD LING

ST ANTHONY OF PADUA

Friend of all the world

ST PAULS

Acknowledgements: I should like to thank the Chairman and Staff of the Franciscan Study Centre at the University of Kent for their friendly help, and Fr Kevin Ward, SCA, for answering so promptly all the questions I put to him.

Cover design by Mary Lou Winters fsp; illustration reproduced by kind permission of Messengers of St Anthony, Padua

ST PAULS
Middlegreen, Slough SL3 6BT, United Kingdom
Moyglare Road, Maynooth, Co. Kildare, Ireland

© ST PAULS (UK) 1995

ISBN 085439 503 2

Set by TuKan, High Wycombe
Printed by The Guernsey Press Co. Ltd, Guernsey, C.I.

ST PAULS is an activity of the priests and brothers of the
Society of St Paul who proclaim the Gospel through the media
of social communication

Contents

*For Michael Bettaney, translator and friend,
and Peter, but for whom...*

Introduction

St Anthony of Padua was not from Padua, and his name was not Anthony. And no-one starts out as a saint. His evolution is a fascinating story, from its beginning eight hundred years ago in the Portuguese port of Lisbon, to the world-wide cult of the present day.

Whenever you go inside older churches, you find the statue of an impossibly ethereal young man in a brown Franciscan habit, balancing a small child seated on an open book; his other arm supports a sheaf of lilies. There are votive candles flickering, sometimes tablets bearing the thanks of his clients, and always a receptacle for alms for his poor.

When his name is mentioned, people respond to it with a very special smile. Their devotion is obvious, but there is something secretive about it. Gradually you realise that any number of them believe that St Anthony is their own particular saint – exclusive, and yet somehow shared. Clients of his are a brotherhood and sisterhood that stretches around the world.

All varieties of Christians may be counted among his devotees, and some who can hardly be called Christian at all, because he reaches a level of consciousness that existed in pagan times. The Church is distrustful of anything that disturbs her careful differentiation between the acceptance of the miraculous and mere superstition, yet she canonised St Anthony by popular demand, and his cult has her blessing. Indeed, for many he is the only link they have with the spiritual life.

Most of his favours, though by no means all, are small ones. These are the kind people talk about readily – the car keys located, the parking places obtained, the spectacles

9

that appear when least expected and most needed – these are the daily miracles. Often there is an element of humour in them, as things that are lost resurface in an incongruous context; but he is consulted on great occasions too, at turning-points in life. Then you meet reticence; the desire to speak of such incidents is confined to rare moments with the most intimate friends. He is the patron of lovers, and pregnant women, as well as the picker-up of trifles; he is the comfort of travellers, and a resort in illness. He is a saint of all work, just as he was a man of all work.

In these pages, I have tried to find that man behind the Wonder Worker, the Doctor of the Church who spends his eternity hunting mislaid articles, rewarded by loose change. But we cannot dismiss the Wonder Worker, as they tried to do at the turn of the century when it was thought that Science had to explain everything according to its own laws. Scientists are now mature enough to admit that there are areas in which they are baffled, where there are no answers to questions posed by their observations of the universe – in fact some of their findings leave more room for miracles. The dances of protons and neutrons, the presence or absence of a gene are physically small things, and divine intervention seems easy. Perhaps all miracles are small miracles; they certainly are, set against the stupendous miracle of creation.

There are some people who generate great strength and energy, and seem to have power not only over others, but over matter. It almost seems an arbitrary gift, for it is given to all kinds of people, not by any means confined to the virtuous. They are healers, and mediums – preachers, and con men – saints and dictators. There will be times in this narrative of St Anthony's life when you may believe that he was that kind of person, though he himself said that the age of miracles had passed with the time of the apostles. Yet wherever he went odd things were reported as happening around him, which others designated miraculous, but which he seems to have taken completely for granted.

You may speculate about the purpose of these interruptions in the ordinary course of events, but they gave a great deal of pleasure to their recipients, and created faith in their witnesses. Perhaps that is sufficient reason for them, since in that way they show the power of the Holy Spirit.

In his lifetime, St Anthony's power was more important to other people than it was to him. He used it sparingly, out of sheer good nature, simply because people asked him. Very few have excelled him in humility.

Apart from the wonders, he is an attractive figure, quite content to play second fiddle to the great St Francis and St Dominic. In the Church's history he comes between them and the intellectual flowering of St Bonaventure and St Thomas Aquinas. He was a model keeper of the promises he made at the age of fifteen – poverty, chastity and obedience – a good monk, and later a good friar. He neither sought nor evaded his fame, enduring it as he endured physical illness, without complaint. May we join with his friends all over the world in saying: "Blessed St Anthony, pray for us."

The making of a canon

In the thirteenth century, the great seaport of Lisbon, where St Anthony was born, was on the edge of the known world. It was popularly believed to have been founded by Ulysses during his wanderings, which gave it an almost legendary quality for the people of the time. From its harbour, ships laden with wine, textiles, olive oil, fish and the fine works of Portuguese silversmiths sailed to supply the cities of the Mediterranean and North Africa.

Long before, it had attracted the attention of the warriors of Islam. In the seventh century they had swarmed up from Syria and colonised Europe almost as far as Northern France. With them, they brought the culture they had taken over from the Greeks. They were warmly welcomed, as they put an end to the multiple taxes exacted by their imperial masters, and replaced them with a single tax that did not hamper trade.

They left the mark of their civilisation on Lisbon; architecture based on the mosques, stained glass, metalwork, the practice of medicine and the writing of lyric poetry. Intellectually and technologically, they were superior to the Christian nations they conquered, but made no attempt to prevent them from worshipping as they wished. They allowed Jews an equal freedom, and the three religions coexisted happily for centuries. Indeed, their prophet had taken over many Christian doctrines; the unity and omnipotence of God, his personal nature and creative power, the fall of Lucifer, and the individual responsibility for actions in this life that would earn heaven or hell in an eternal future. The big difference – and it was enormous – was that Islam denied the divinity of Jesus, the existence of the Trinity, the Eucharist, and its celebration by the priesthood.

All might have been well if the Turks had not wrested Jerusalem from the more pacific Moslems who originated in Egypt; the Turks were altogether less tolerant, harassing Christian pilgrims to the Holy Places. This was a calamity, as great spiritual favours were gained by making the journey, and hardened sinners travelled to Palestine as an act of penance. To ensure their safety, Pope Urban II called on Christendom to unite in an effort to oust the Turks.

The response was a ferment of religious zeal. Kings and overlords turned from fighting each other to answer the Pope's appeal. Their civilisation was held together by oaths of loyalty between monarch and subject, lord and vassal. One of the obligations was military service, and the crusading armies were composed of close-knit clusters of men coming from the same rural districts. While the protagonists were away, those left behind escaped from this feudal structure and drifted off into the towns. There they owed allegiance to no man, and could strengthen their influence by joining the flourishing craft guilds. This was the background against which society ebbed and flowed through Lisbon's narrow streets.

The reconquest of the city was achieved in 1147 when Alphonse I, who had recently become the Christian king of Portugal, invited Crusaders from England, France and Germany, sailing by his territory, to assist him in driving out the Moors, promising them rich rewards. The Crusaders overran the city, looting and attacking innocent bystanders. Heavy penalties were exacted, the least of which was tarring and feathering. Eventually they were confined to their ships, but they soon broke out and ran amok again.

The King ordered that they should be imprisoned until their leaders gave guarantees of good conduct, and made restitution to the local shopkeepers and householders. It must have been a great relief when they sailed away to resume their Crusade. But the Moors still had a grip on the Iberian Peninsular, and the raids continued. It was a turbulent time, for the Church as well as the temporal power. There were still pious souls in all walks of life, many of whom figured in St Anthony's story, alongside priests and even bishops who lived in open concubinage, practised usury, and left the Church for more lucrative posts in secular service. These were readily available, as although many of the small parishes were served by unlettered priests, the clergy tended to be the best educated members of society.

It is generally accepted that St Anthony's birth took place in 1195, on the feast of the Assumption, August 15th; certainly he was devoted to Our Lady. The early chroniclers give his name as 'Fernando de Bulloens' – which they also spelled 'Bouillon', in an attempt to relate him to a famous Crusader who had helped in the first capture of Jerusalem. The same sources name his father as Martin de Bulloens, and his mother Maria Teresa Tavera; apparently they lived in some splendour, near the West Door of the Cathedral. Very little of the old city survived the earthquakes to which the region is subject, but the font in which the baby Fernando was probably baptised still exists. Details of his parents' lives have vanished almost without trace, though a tablet in the church of St Vincent de Fora claims to mark his mother's resting-place. An Infanta of Portugal who met Fernando later remembered him as the son of 'ordinary citizens', while a lawyer of Padua who met him after he was acclaimed as a preacher described him as a nobleman – but what appeared ordinary to the Infanta might have seemed noble to the notary. Like much of Fernando's early life, it is a matter of conjecture.

In the Cathedral there is a statue of him, robed as an altar-boy, and there is a strong tradition that he participated in the Mass. Normally the laity congregated in the nave and could see very little until the Host was elevated at the consecration. As an acolyte, Fernando would have been close to the sacred mysteries, and this may have caused the first stirrings of a vocation.

Several legends of his early years have been handed down. If they have a basis in fact, they appear to indicate that the very special power he had went back to his beginnings. Some children seem to be in touch with a power deeper and more fundamental than the ordinary business of the adult world. Most of them forget how to reach it as they grow up and lose the beautiful clarity of childhood, but not St Anthony. It is told of him that he was on a farm owned by his family at a place called Sé Mamedé, and his father asked him to scare birds away from a field, nearly ripe for harvesting. Fernando wished to pray in a derelict chapel nearby, and called to the birds to perch in a tree and await his return, so the field was left untouched. He would always try to balance his obligations and responsibilities with his need for contemplation.

On another occasion he met a small girl who had been sent to fetch water from a well. She had tripped and smashed her newly-filled jug, and the water would have been almost as precious as the receptacle in the summers of that arid land. Anxious about her reception at home, she was in great distress, and the sight aroused the sympathy Anthony always felt for the downtrodden. He picked up the pieces and as if by magic handed her the jug – whole and serviceable again. But he was not a magician who can convince people by sleight-of-hand that he has power over material things. The boy Fernando could, when he wanted to, mend the broken, as he evidently did in this case.

The following story is a great favourite with many of the early chroniclers and with the people of Lisbon, who locate it in several of their churches. The most frequently-told version takes place in the Cathedral when Fernando was kneeling on the steps leading from the nave into the choir. A large dog bounded up and thoroughly shocked him. Believing it to be the devil, he traced the sign of the cross on the step before him; when the animal left, the sign of the cross remained imprinted in the marble. This may be a case of the medieval mind seeing the devil prowling everywhere, as it saw God everywhere in creation, and a small boy might well have been frightened by a fierce dog – though in some accounts the dog disappears and becomes the psychological threat of a powerful temptation. In any case, Fernando must have been a remarkable child, to have such a tale told about him.

His presence in the Cathedral was not only because of its proximity to his home, or duties at the altar. From the age of about seven, he also attended the school held in rooms off the cloisters. The Cathedral had been built by Gilbert of Hastings, an Englishman who was Bishop of Lisbon from the time of its liberation, and the school he founded was probably run on English lines. Most of the time would have been taken up with acquiring Latin, the language of the universal Church and the key to its treasures of learning. This was taught by studying the psalms and other liturgical texts. It must be kept in mind that all the texts were copied by hand, and these would be the ones commonly used. The most popular grammars were those of Donatus and Priscian, and these would be passed among the boys, since most of the learning was by rote.

At the age of fifteen, when most families were thinking of finding marriage partners for their children, Fernando informed his parents that he had other plans for his future. He wished to join the Canons Regular.

Founded in 1062, they were something between an old order like the Benedictines and the secular clergy. They had the care of parishes and seminaries, but they were encouraged by the Pope to take vows of poverty, chastity and obedience like monks, and he had enjoined on them the Rule outlined by St Augustine, adopted in 1139, from his experience of living in community at Hippo in North Africa in the fifth century.

There is some evidence that it was not Fernando's wish that he should join the Canons at their nearest foundation, St Vincent de Fora, only about a mile outside the walls of Lisbon, but his family might well have exerted pressure on him not to move too far away.

Fernando was never one to do anything by halves, and he meant to keep both the letter and the spirit of the Rule. It was founded on mutual love, expressed in community of possessions, and the virtue of humility. Everything was shared, and nobody claimed anything as his own. As a rich young man, he would have put his worldly goods into the common purse. He was required not to look down on the brothers who had been of lower social status than himself. As the Rule put it: 'What good is it to dispense gifts to the poor, if giving up riches makes a person prouder than he was when he had a fortune?'

The young Fernando was encouraged to persevere in prayer, to think of the meaning of the words of the psalms and hymns when singing the Divine Office, and keep to their precise text. Meals in common were accompanied by readings to discourage superficial conversation. Once a week the reading was from the Rule, so that the brothers would be constantly reminded of its provisions and recognised where they fell short. Fasting was strict, but tempered in the case of infirmity, and those entering who were used to a comfortable life received extra nourishment until they could do without it; Fernando might well have qualified for this mitigation. The same exception was made for the sick, but the brothers were never allowed to murmur if the privilege was not extended to them. They were not allowed to go out unaccompanied, as they had to report each other's infractions of the Rule. Simplicity of life was emphasised as best suited to servants of God.

They were concerned for the welfare of the sick amongst them, and the brothers were to report any illness. If they suffered from an ailment with no external symptoms, the brother's word was to be trusted. There was to be no quarrelling. If one brother offended another, amends had to be made swiftly, and the offended must be equally quick to forgive. An exception would be made in the correcting of someone as young as Fernando. Discipline had to be preserved, and it was considered better to beg pardon of God than undermine authority by begging pardon of the young. The Superior had to be obeyed as a father. Given the extensive parental rights of the time, this was no light command, though the Superior was urged to try and rule by love rather than fear; it was pointed out that love and respect were equally necessary.

St Vincent de Fora was a pleasant place, with a view of the River Tagus, and it had been built by Alphonse I as a chantry for the repose of the souls of the Crusaders who were killed in the Siege of Lisbon. It also carried on the work of teaching the catechism, preaching, almsgiving at stated hours for the needy of the city, and the direction of a hospice for pilgrims. Study was a regular duty for Augustinian Canons, and Fernando showed every sign of becoming a brilliant scholar. The great drawback for him about such a congenial place, was its close proximity to old friends who insisted on putting in an appearance and distracting him from his aim – which was no less than a perfect performance of the Rule, and union with God.

After two years, when he must still have been a novice, he therefore distanced himself from these unwelcome visitors by asking to be removed to the mother-house of Santa Cruz, a hundred miles away in Coimbra. This was the capital city of the young kingdom of Portugal, and in its castle fortress lived the King, whose corpulence led his subjects to refer to him as Alphonse the Fat. This may suggest a jovial individual, but in fact he was bad-tempered and avaricious, grudging the legacies left by his father to his brothers and sisters. They had to threaten him with the vengeance of the Pope, but despite this the business was not settled until 1216, after a Papal investigation.

The Pope in question was Innocent III, who had taken his place in Peter's chair when Fernando was a child, and did not hesitate to challenge the temporal powers who opposed his policies, warring amongst themselves to the detriment of their people. King Alphonse was no exception, seizing church goods and imprisoning bishops who spoke out against him.

The monastery of Santa Cruz, with its beautiful Gothic church and exquisitely carved figures over the West Door, still exists, and contains the tiny cell of St Anthony. It had been founded with seventy-two Canons in 1132, before its liberation, and Alphonse I had given a grant of money to enable the Canons to study abroad. One of them went to the community of Avignon to study their interpretation of the Rule. He brought back the idea of chanting the anthems, and several valuable manuscripts for the library, including St Augustine's commentary on St John, St Bede's commentary on St Luke, and works concerning the Gospels of St Matthew and St Luke; the Hexameron, the Pastoral, and a book concerning Penance by Ambrose, the great saint of Milan, who received St Augustine into the Church.

Santa Cruz was wealthy. By running their communities with an eye to self-sufficiency, and some generous gifts from rich patrons anxious to buy their way into heaven, the Canons' estates were commercially sound, with all the temptations that such success brought in its train. This, and a high reputation for learning, attracted both the best and worst recruits to the foundation.

The first Prior was exemplary; St Theotonius, a friend of St Bernard of Clairvaux, the great Carthusian reformer and theologian. In his later years, Theotonius was proud to lean on a stick given him by the saint. His rule over Santa Cruz lasted for twenty years, and he left it in such good order that it was an oasis of civilisation.

After his death in 1154, the next holder of the office, Prior John, was a very different kettle of fish. The year before Fernando joined the community in 1212 Pope Innocent III had written of insinuations and rumours that had reached him, concerning the Prior. He had been accused of squandering the goods of the monastery and been excommunicated. Things were no better in the bishopric, as the Pope had to rebuke the bishop for not being a shepherd to his flock, because he had sided with the King against the Church. These were the men to whom Fernando had vowed obedience.

If Fernando's idealism about the religious life did not become tinged with cynicism, it was simply because his personality was too sanguine – though he did say later: 'The wicked Superior beats on the back, that is the patience, of his subject. To the Superior, such persecution brings ruin, but to the subject an eternal reward.'

There is a wealth of experience behind his words which suggests he was no stranger to discipline inflicted unjustly and maliciously, and had found his own way of dealing with it.

In 1213 the Fourth Lateran Council made arrangements for the inspection of monasteries. The assessors were empowered to institute reforms and inform the Holy See if Priors or Abbots were unsuitable. It may have been a coincidence, but within two years Prior John had retired to a hermitage on account of his advanced age, only to be succeeded by his nephew. In happier times the Pope had granted the privilege of complete independence to Santa Cruz, allowing the Prior to be subject only to the Holy See, and stating that no Canon could be released from the monastery except by permission of the Prior – or, more unusually, the entire community.

The Canons 'vowed in a special manner to study with the particular aim of rendering themselves more fit for the service of God and souls, and to prepare them, if they had sufficient aptitude, to fulfil pastoral functions in the Church.' The pastoral functions included saying Mass at several churches they administered, preaching homilies and hearing confessions, and Fernando was trained to perform these offices. Though the year of his ordination is unknown it is fairly certain to have taken place before he made the next great step in his career.

There is said to have been a manuscript written in 1222 and originating in Santa Cruz which states: 'Among the Canons Regular of Santa Cruz at that time was the Reverend Father Anthony, whose name was Fernando Martini' – (son of Martin) – 'a very learned and pious man, much distinguished in letters, and illustrious by the abundance of his merits.' That such a paragon would have been raised to the priesthood is more than likely.

A story is told which seems to belong to his period in the noviciate. He was sweeping the cloister outside the church – the Canons were bound by the Rule to undertake menial labour as part of their day – and he wished very much to be present at the Mass taking place within. He fell on his knees as the bell sounded for the consecration; the wall he was facing appeared to melt away, and he saw the priest elevating the host. Similar things are reported about other saints, including St Clare, who was living at the same time. This was not to be St Anthony's only link with her.

But it was in his studies that he impressed everyone. We know many of the books he read, because he quoted them in later life. His greatest debt was to St Augustine, whose Rule he knew so well and lived from day to day; at this time the Canons Regular had the charge of the body of the saint, and he was deeply revered within the Order. Among St Augustine's works was a great treatise on the Holy Trinity, and an exposition of Divine Grace. His long book, 'The City of God', was read extensively by scholars and theologians, and Fernando would certainly have studied it. No stranger to violence himself, he would appreciate that it was written during the time that Alaric the Goth rampaged through Italy. When the Roman Empire broke up and it seemed an entire civilisation was about to vanish, Augustine, then Bishop of Hippo in North Africa, sat down to write a book which he knew might never survive to be read. Such an act of faith would have appealed to the young student.

Augustine has endeared himself to subsequent generations by the frankness of his Confessions and the story of his acceptance of Catholicism, which is one of the most moving accounts in the whole history of conversion. His story of temptations overcome and worldly ambitions renounced was an inspiration to those who followed. His fight against the Manichees, amongst whom he had been numbered for a time, and the Arians who denied Christ's divinity, was a pattern for writers and preachers against heresy. A prayer – the 'Te solum amo' – which he made in his characteristic rhythmical prose must have found an echo in the heart of Fernando –

'Now I love Thee alone,
Thee alone do I follow,
Thee alone do I seek,
Thee alone I am ready to serve.
For Thou alone hast just dominion,
Under Thy sway I long to be.
This only do I ask of Thy extreme kindness
That Thou convert me wholly to Thee
And allow nothing to prevent me
From wending my way to Thee.'

But he read widely, and among the writers he later
quoted was St Jerome, the author of the Biblical translation, the Latin Vulgate, used extensively in the Middle
Ages. Jerome was not only a scholar and a beloved teacher;
in his retreat near Bethlehem, he was famous for his knowledge of classic rhetorical models and an imitator of their
powers of invective. Fernando also studied St Isadore, a
fighter against Arianism and writer on many subjects be-
sides religion, including history and science. His extensive
encyclopaedia of the knowledge of his time, the latter part
of the sixth and first half of the seventh century, was used
as a textbook in the thirteenth. In his 'Paradiso', the great
poet Dante put him in the company of the English historian
St Bede, whose work was also studied by Fernando.

Two more of the four great Latin Doctors – St Ambrose
and St Gregory – were known to the young Canon;
St Ambrose's hymns and of course the Athanasian Creed
would have been very familiar to him, also his sermons and
lessons on the catechism. St Gregory the Great, the first
Pope to call himself 'The servant of the servants of God',
was Fernando's model for the duties of pastoral care.
St John Damascene who lived in the seventh century, in the
wilderness between Jerusalem and the Dead Sea, provided
him with a summary of Christian doctrine as expounded by
the Greek fathers, and he seems to have known his sermons
on the Assumption of our Lady.

Origen, an even earlier Father from the second century,

23

would have given him a taste of Platonic, Pythagorean and Stoic thought, as well as Christian apologetics. He may also have been acquainted with Cassiodorus's 'Institutiones', a study course for the monks of the Vivarium, written in the sixth century; the library seems to have contained various bestiaries and books on natural science.

But above and beyond all these, he studied the Scriptures. We do not know whether, like St Bonaventure several decades later, he wrote out the whole bible twice, but he not only read it and meditated upon it – he learned it by heart. It was said of him that if all the sacred manuscripts were destroyed, he could have replaced them from memory. What he read in Coimbra, he retained for the rest of his life. It almost argues that he had the medieval equivalent of a photographic memory – although it was more likely to have been aural rather than visual. Most authors in the days of hand-written manuscripts dictated their work, writing being considered a mechanical chore, and they were probably read aloud in the same way. He cemented his power of recall with ingenious methods of reference, breaking words up into their component letters, cross-indexing them with their Latin and Greek meanings, and drawing idiosyncratic images from them.

An early biographer said of him: 'Once he had transferred to Coimbra, he cultivated his intelligence through assiduous study and exercised his soul through meditation. Night and day, whenever the opportunity arose, he continued his study of the scriptures. Through reading the texts containing historical truth, his faith was strengthened by allegorical comparisons; while applying the words of scripture to himself, his demeanour showed the disposition of his soul. As he scrutinised the meaning within the divine words with healthy curiosity, the scriptural witness acted to strengthen his intellect against lapses into error. With diligent research, he also reflected on the thought of the saints.'

In this way the mind of Father Fernando was formed into an instrument that would make known the word of God. For St Augustine, the master of rhetoric, intended that study should be translated into evangelisation. At that time, Fernando had limited opportunities. His voice was not heard beyond Coimbra, as he served the churches there, preaching homilies to the courtiers of Alphonse the Fat, and the townspeople who satisfied their appetite for luxury. But there was one person at court with a feeling for the spiritual life, and she had more influence than any other women in the land – Alphonse's wife, Queen Urraca. It was the Queen who decided something was needed to enhance her natural piety, and an act of hers that led Fernando to undertake an adventure that would alter his congenial way of life, his status – even his name – and take him away from Lisbon for ever.

The making of a friar

We have seen how Fernando's monastery had been affected by the corruption of its Prior. That situation was often repeated throughout the year 1210; the established Orders had paid the price of success and become wealthy, losing the true sense of their vows of poverty. When this happened, chastity and obedience often disappeared too. Fernando, who was aspiring to perfection in the religious life, needed guidance and help that were not forthcoming at Santa Cruz – but there was a movement afoot that would satisfy his need.

One February morning in Assisi on the feast of St Matthias, the disciple who replaced Judas among the apostles, a Gospel according to St Matthew was read in the derelict chapel called the Portiuncula, or 'Little Porch'. It was the account of Christ's call to his disciples to go out and preach the Good News, taking nothing with them – no shoes, no extra tunic, no staff, and no money – especially no money. The words went home most particularly to one of the hearers, Francis Bernardone. He had already dedicated his life to the service of Lady Poverty; it was his custom to personalise things that others saw as abstractions, and he embraced her like a lover.

He could hardly wait for the Mass to be over, to obey the call. The fact that he was a layman and had no business to preach at all failed to deter him. He went to a place where people forgathered and began to speak. Anyone else might have been hampered by lack of experience or embarrassment, but he was so much on fire with the love of God that he did naturally what was to take another man years to learn – the secret of letting the words come from his heart. He went on until his voice failed, and then the crowd

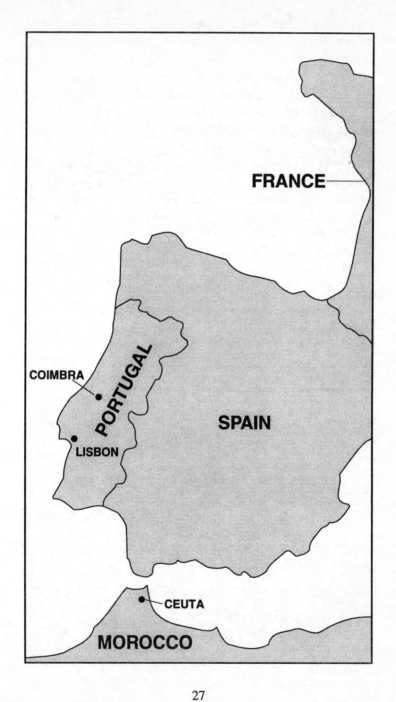

whose curiosity had made them stop and listen gradually drifted away. But three men stayed behind and approached him.

One of them, Bernardo di Quintavalle, was rich, and like the others he wanted to share Francis's way of life. When he asked how he should do it Francis gave him Our Lord's answer to the wealthy young man who wanted to follow him: 'Sell all you have and give it to the poor.' The following morning, Francis gained further confirmation of this advice when they opened the book of the Gospels at random, and found the text again. Bernardo was more generous than the biblical young man, and responded by giving away all he owned. He was not the only one; in a few months, the little band numbered twelve. In the monastic life poverty was obligatory, as each monk's worldly goods were shared out, but Francis proposed something new; for him poverty meant that no-one should own anything. The Brothers would beg for food when they could not earn it by manual labour. Their house – a tumbledown hut near the Portiuncula, dedicated to Our Lady of the Angels – they rented from some Benedictines in exchange for a basket of fish they caught themselves.

But to preach the Gospel, as they felt called to do, they had to have approval from the Church. The nearest authority, the Bishop of Assisi, advised them to join one of the established Orders, but Francis did not want to give up the idea of a new kind of Order that could travel the world, unencumbered by possessions. They put together a form of Rule comprising these revolutionary proposals, and prepared to set off for Rome to appeal to Pope Innocent III. Before they left, they elected a leader; surprisingly, they chose Bernardo, and Francis accepted the lower place with joy.

Their first encounter with the young reforming Pope was a failure. He decided that their proposed Rule was more than human endurance could stand; nobody would be able to live up to it. It was considered better to temper the Rule, rather than fail constantly to measure up to such a high ideal. Francis was convinced that he and his followers were called by God and would be helped by Him, and the Pope stopped short of sending them away empty-handed. There was something about the ragged band that led him to allow them to make a second appeal. In a dream, he saw the Lateran Basilica tumbling down, upheld on the back of a small figure in a tattered tunic whom he recognised as Francis.

It was well over a thousand years since Jesus had left the earth and the young Church had been founded at Pentecost. There seemed to be no-one to carry on the work of the apostles, to admonish vice and applaud virtue. It was worth taking a chance on this motley collection of Brothers; especially Francis, with his shining zeal and the humility to take second place among them. Pope Innocent gave them permission to preach wherever the Bishop of the diocese would allow it, and he appointed Francis as leader. About the Rule he kept discreetly silent; there would be time enough to see how that worked out in practise. With the long-sought papal approval, Francis went back joyfully to Assisi, and his example appealed to men of all classes and conditions who asked to join him.

It was not only men who were called. Clare Offreduccio was almost the same age as Fernando de Bulloens. She too was well-born, for she belonged to one of the most prominent families in Assisi, and Francis had enabled her to elope from her father's house and embrace a new life of poverty, chastity and obedience, as the first member of the Order familiarly known as the 'Poor Clares'. The story appealed to the taste of the time as a variant on the theme of courtly love, and many like-minded women joined her. It was an enclosed Order, and the nuns spent their time in forming a powerhouse of prayer for those in the world outside, and more especially for the mendicant friars.

Knowing Francis had changed Clare's life. Although it would be a long time before Fernando actually saw him, his influence was beginning to be felt, even in Coimbra.

Francis sent his friars around Italy, two by two. The

result was a phenomenal increase in numbers. In 1216 they held their first General Chapter at the Portiuncula, and it was decided that they should travel all over Europe. The following year they reached Spain and Portugal. In Spain they were accused of heresy, but although at first they were considered rather too rough and unsophisticated for the Portuguese, when two of them, Zachary and Gauthier, appeared at the court of Coimbra to ask the Bishop for permission to preach, as they were bound to do, they won over Queen Urraca and her sister-in-law, Princess Sancia, who gave them land to build a convent. With this royal blessing, they became the fashion, but refused to allow it to alter their resolution to live as the poorest of the poor. The convent, about a mile outside the city, was a collection of huts, probably made of reeds and olive branches. The place was known as 'St Anthony of the Olives'. Whether it acquired the name before or after Fernando was connected with it is a matter of conjecture, but its foundation was decisive for his future.

He might well have met the Friars Minor and heard their stories, because there is a strong tradition that he had acted as Hosteller at Santa Cruz. It was the Hosteller's duty to keep the guests' quarters spotless, with clean clothes provided for travellers, towels, mattresses, blankets and sheets not only clean but not torn, and the quilts had to be the right size to cover the beds – they would have passed muster with the most fastidious hospital manager. Equal care had to be taken with eating utensils; the metal basins had to be polished, the cups without cracks and the salt-cellars kept clean and filled. If the guests wanted to write, candles, candlesticks and writing materials had to be provided. Keys, locks and bolts were to keep the place safe from intruders; it had to be ensured that the fire did not smoke, and the whole guest-house had to be kept free from spiders webs and dirt, and strewn with fresh rushes. Considering the primitive nature of the cleaning materials available, it was a formidable task.

At Santa Cruz, Fernando would welcome the friars who

came to beg alms. By this time they had become a familiar sight on the roads, along with pilgrims, pedlars and other itinerants, and they kept the news flowing from city to city and country to country. Among other things, they told of the accession of a new Pope, Honorius III in place of their old friend Innocent III. Three years later, in 1219, Honorius called upon priests to show a desire for martyrdom by going to preach among the Saracens; he wanted men who would thank God for the privilege of offering Him their lives.

Francis welcomed the call and recommended his Brothers to witness the faith to the Moslems, by acting as their servants and confessing their faith. He hoped to evangelise the Moslems by teaching the elements of Christianity. In his directive he repeated Jesus's words that 'He who loses his life for my sake will save it until life everlasting' and quoted the Beatitude: 'Blessed are those who are persecuted for righteousness' sake, for theirs is the kingdom of heaven.'

The Friars at the Chapter of 1219 had been selected by Francis, who said to them: 'My sons, God has commanded me to send you to the land of the Saracens to preach and confess His faith, and to combat the law of Mohamet. I myself will go elsewhere to labour for the conversion of the infidel, and it is my intention to send missionaries throughout the world. Prepare yourselves then, to fulfil the will of God.' They immediately answered: 'We are ready, O Father, to obey you in all things', and Francis blessed them, saying: 'May the blessing of God the Father descend upon you as it descended upon the Apostles; may he strengthen you, guide you, console you in your tribulations; fear not, for the Lord is with you, and with you will strongly fight.'

But it was not in Brother Francis's character to send others to what might be their deaths without setting a good example. He had been thwarted of martyrdom previously in 1212; first by a terrible storm that had carried the ship he sailed in ashore at Ancona on the Adriatic – then he changed direction and tried to go to Morocco by way of Spain and was struck down by an illness that prevented him from proceeding further. It was 'Brother Ass', as he called his body, striking back after the austerities he had inflicted upon himself.

Nothing daunted, he made a third attempt immediately after the Chapter of 1219 and arrived at Damietta in the August of that year, when the Crusaders were besieging the port. He foresaw the devastation of the city and deplored the deterioration of the fine spirit of the earlier Christian armies, doing his best to warn them that they were no longer fighting for a worthy cause, but they only laughed at him. He could not bear to watch the ensuing battle, but sent one of his companions to bring back news of the outcome. Ever compassionate, he mourned over the carnage.

During a lull in the fighting, although the Saracens had beaten him and held him up to ridicule, he confronted their leader, Melek-El-Kamil, quite unafraid. What could they do to a man who positively welcomed death threats, and was so steeped in humility that no-one could insult him? Melek-El-Kamil, after a vain attempt to bribe him, listened to his exposition of the Christian faith and asked him to pray that God would make known which of their two beliefs was most pleasing to him.

On their way to Morocco, five of the Brothers passed through Coimbra. Their names, ever remembered in the history of the Order of Friars Minor, were Berard, Peter and Otho, with two lay Brothers, Adjuto and Accursio. If Fernando did not meet them, he certainly heard of their intention to seek martyrdom. The news that Pope Honorius had asked for clemency for Christians falling into Moslem hands had probably not reached them; it would have frustrated men who desired nothing but death from their captors. Their white-hot determination generated an equally warm enthusiasm in the Queen, although Alphonse's brother Don Pedro was the Commander-In-Chief of a Moslem army, having taken refuge in Morocco after a family feud.

The five Brothers reached Seville, which was still held

by Moslems; the ruler paid no attention to them and passed them on to Abu Jacob in Morocco – the Emir whom Don Pedro served. It was Abu Jacob who advised them not to provoke the Mohammedans, but on coming into the presence of the Emir Father Berard shouted at him: 'Jesus Christ is the true God, Mohammed is nothing but an impostor!' Anything more calculated to provoke his hearers can hardly be imagined, but Abu Jacob was tolerant of what seemed to him lunatic behaviour, and merely banished them from his territory, ordering his minions to escort them to Ceuta, the nearest port to Europe. They escaped before they could be put on a boat, returned to Morocco, and immediately set about preaching, in order to get themselves arrested again.

Fearing their disruptive effect on his people, Abu Jacob could only play into their hands, and tried to starve them into submission, but they were well used to fasting and after twenty days without food they were more defiant than ever. This caused riots against them in the city, and Abu Jacob's patience was exhausted. He allowed them to be subjected to cruel torture that left their bodies torn and bleeding, but their morale was as high as ever; they refused to take advantage of offers of freedom if they would desist from preaching. The Emir gave way at last and in a frenzy of rage even assisted in their beheading. An incensed crowd threw the bodies into a refuse pit at the edge of the city.

Christian sympathisers crept out under cover of darkness and took possession of their remains; Don Pedro, to make amends for his failure to prevent their fate, put these into two bejewelled caskets and accompanied them as far as Galicia. There were probably political reasons for his not taking them all the way to Coimbra, as he seems to have delegated a knight of his entourage to complete the journey.

Coimbra was in a ferment at the thought of the reception of their dead heroes; reports of miracles obtained by merely viewing the relics were commonplace. The whole town turned out, led by Queen Urraca herself, barefoot and with a candle in her hands. Not to be outdone, other members of the court imitated her. The dead friars were honoured as the first martyrs of the Order of Friars Minor, and made it more popular than ever. The church of Santa Cruz was chosen as their temporary resting-place, as the tiny chapel among the rough huts at the Franciscan convent was too small to accommodate the number of pilgrims that began to arrive.

No doubt the community kept vigil – amongst then, Fernando – and in the watches of the night a profound change came over him; one might almost call it a conversion. All the comfort and security of his position as a Canon Regular became as nothing beside the crown these unlettered, generous souls had won. He had always been a perfectionist in his observance of the Rule, but here was another Rule which they had followed with a deeper perfection. He must have sought solitude to think through the call he was beginning to hear.

No doubt his mind turned to another conversion – that of St Augustine, his guide and mentor across the centuries. In the depths of a torment that was both physical and mental, Augustine had turned to a friend and asked: 'What ails us? What have you heard? The unlearned arise and take heaven by force; and we with our learning are heartless – look how we wallow in flesh and blood. Is it because they have preceded us that we are ashamed to follow, or is it because we are not ashamed that we do not at least follow?' Then, bursting into tears and wishing to weep in secret, he went out into the garden.

Fernando, who never forgot anything he had read, recalled that St Augustine wrote in his 'Confessions' that it was of St Anthony of Egypt, the Desert Father, that he had thought at this crucial moment. For on the brink of his own conversion, St Anthony had walked into a church when the gospel was being read, and had taken the words as binding upon himself – and the message was: 'Go and sell all that you have and give to the poor, and you shall have treasure in heaven... Come, and follow me.'

This was the oracle that had converted Anthony, and

Augustine felt it was directed at him too – but what was wonderful to Fernando was that this was the same text that Francis and his first companions had found when they opened the Gospels for guidance at the very beginning of their quest for perfection.

Fernando no longer had any wealth of his own, but he had a heart and mind to give to the poor, and he could leave the shelter of Santa Cruz for the mission field, where he would give his life – the only treasure he had left – for Christ. It would have been easy for him to contact the friars, since they did not move far from the remains of their fellow Franciscans. In those days, piety took strange forms, and there were those who would try to steal such precious relics.

Fernando waited for a suitable opportunity, and then asked, in the words of the old chronicles: 'My very dear brothers, I would gladly assume the habit of your Order if you would promise to send me directly after my entrance among you to the country of the Saracens; thus I should acquire the same merits as your holy martyrs and share their crown.'

This was language the friars could understand; the language of Francis, touching a chord within the humblest member of the Order. They sensed that he was a romantic like themselves, a troubadour who would approach death with a song. The Friars Minor had only recently instituted a noviciate – too recently to be established so far from their meeting-place at the Portiuncula – and there was nothing to prevent Fernando from being accepted simply and promptly, just as the earliest brothers had been received. But there was one more bridge still to be crossed, and that was an important one.

He could be prevented through the provision made by Innocent III that any Canon who wished to leave Santa Cruz had to obtain permission from the Prior and the entire community. There would have been a solemn meeting in the Chapter House, an interrogation and very probably a ballot. Perhaps Fernando tried to outline the steps he had travelled and managed to convince them that the moment when he became Franciscan was when he had been most truly Augustinian. The young Canon pleading his case must have melted the opposition, for the desired permission was given, and he abandoned his white habit, black cowl and leather belt, for the rough tunic and knotted cord of a Friar Minor.

Did he think as he parted with the cowl of the time when as Infirmarian, he put it on a sick Canon who was cured not only of his illness but also great temptations of the devil? Whatever the feelings of the community, one at least held a grudge against him, calling out with acrimony: 'Go, go — for you will become a saint!' Fernando's rejoinder was: 'When you hear I have become holy, praise God for it' — which seems a suitably humble reply.

He appears to have left for the Franciscan convent immediately after the robing ceremony. There remained one further sacrifice, but like most sacrifices it was repaid richly in blessings. He decided to give up the name he had received in the cathedral at Lisbon, by which he had been known among his family and friends and brothers in Christ. He would take a new name to mark his birth to a new life.

It has always been something of a mystery why he chose to be called Anthony, but the stern old Desert Father would have made a splendid Franciscan. He had lived on a single meal of bread a day, with a little salt. The bread was delivered to him twice a year, and by the time a new consignment was due the remainder was either mouldy or hard as wood. He worked for it by weaving baskets from Nile reeds, eventually becoming the patron of the craft, and lived to be a hundred and five, with all his faculties. Fernando was not planning to live at all, but he meant to die as Anthony, and perhaps he also wished to carry something of Augustine with him. It was extremely unusual for a Franciscan to give up his Christian name, although the surname was relinquished and replaced by that of his birthplace, but no-one seems to have objected to Anthony's innovation. There was a further Augustinian connection;

the saint had mentioned in his 'Confessions' that the Apostle of the Gentiles had desired to be called Paul instead of Saul – his previous name – 'as a sign of so great a victory'. Renewed, and robed as a friar, Anthony was ready to depart for the mission field.

The brothers went out as always, two by two, and logic demands that his companion (or 'socius', as they were called) was a like-minded friar of the convent, since there is no evidence that he went elsewhere to find one. A chronicler called Wadding, writing admittedly in the eighteenth century, identifies him with a Brother Philip or Filippino, who before St Francis's death in 1226 had the great privilege of knowing the saint intimately enough to have touched the stigmata. After the next General Chapter he retired to Colombajo near Monte Ilcino, where he was much loved and credited with many miracles. These continued after his death, and he was buried in the Church of St Francis at Monte Ilcino. Whether this Philip, who certainly existed, was Anthony's socius is more problematical, but if he did accompany him to Morocco he must accept much responsibility for what was to happen later.

The great voyage to Africa would have begun at Lisbon, and after rough contact with the Atlantic, the ship must have passed through the Straits of Gibraltar into the Mediterranean, before making landfall at the Moorish port of Ceuta. There is no record of their journey, but Thomas of Celano has left us a vivid picture of Friars in transit, with his description of St Francis's own voyage in search of martyrdom at the hands of the Saracens in 1212.

Francis planned to take a ship to Syria to preach the Christian faith and penance to the infidels; travellers carried their own provisions, and it was usual to bargain for a place on board. He must have managed to pay for his passage, but contrary winds arose and he and his companion, with all their shipmates, were blown across the Adriatic, to the region of Slavonia. The weather was worsening, and the season for making the Mediterranean crossing was coming to an end; the fear that he might be deprived of his hope of travelling to North Africa made him very anxious to return to Italy and begin again.

There was a ship bound for Ancona, and he begged to be allowed to sail on it, but even his strength of personality could not charm the sailors into granting him a passage, for he no longer had anything to barter. However, it took more than that to deter a Friar Minor, and Francis was nothing if not ingenious. He and his socius waited until all was quiet, then slipped on to the boat secretly, stowing away amongst the cargo. There they lay concealed, trusting in Divine Providence. It produced a messenger in the form of a man who evidently knew of their plight and followed them aboard with provisions. Stopping one of the crew, who luckily was pious and discreet, he said: 'Take these things with you and give them faithfully to those poor men hiding on your boat when they have need of them.'

During the voyage, it happened that a great storm arose, and for several days the crew had to row for their lives, consuming all the food they had in store, until only the secret hoard belonging to Francis was left. This was shared out, and seemed to multiply miraculously until everyone was provided for. The crew were so delighted with the friars that, far from being angry with them for stowing away, they acknowledged that it was due to them that Ancona was reached in safety. The account ends: 'When the sailors saw that they had escaped the dangers of the sea through the servant of God, Francis, they thanked almighty God, who always shows himself wonderful and loveable in his servants.' The subsequent history of the expedition was not so happy, for Francis was taken ill and had to return to Italy without setting foot in Syria.

Anthony himself got very little further. No sooner had he reached Ceuta than he too was struck down by illness. It was described as ague, which was the general name for any kind of fever, and was probably a bad bout of malaria which dragged on through the rest of the winter. His loyal socius nursed him, no doubt begging in order to provide the invalid diet and ease his sufferings. Anthony's health was so debilitated that there was no question of any missionary work. There was nothing to be done but make for home as soon as he was well enough to travel. All the hope and confidence he had when he set out had been utterly eroded; he was a failure as a martyr, incapable of living the life of a Friar Minor. He must have been tempted to give up in despair.

When they did find a boat going in the right direction, they had to bargain for their passage. Perhaps Philip was taken on to work as a mariner, while Anthony occupied himself with lighter tasks. The friars took pride in being able to turn their hands to anything, the more menial the better. That was why they were in such contrast to other clerics, who considered themselves better educated and superior in status to ordinary men. But treacherous winds blew them eastwards across the Mediterranean, and they made landfall at Messina in Sicily. They were told of a Franciscan convent about three miles outside the town, and the two companions, barely recovered from their ordeal, sought refuge there.

The ruler of Sicily, the formidable Frederick II, had been forced to neglect his kingdom while he was occupied with wars in Germany and the mainland of Italy, and had only recently returned as King and Emperor. He had been tutored by two Popes at the dying wish of his mother, Constance of Aragon, and was bereaved of both parents by the age of four, when Pope Innocent II was made Regent of Sicily. The new Emperor was not at all like his famous grandfather, Frederick Barbarossa, who towered over most of his contemporaries, but he tried to model himself upon him, using exercises to build up his poor physique.

Brilliantly clever, he used his skill in languages to manipulate the diplomats at his court. His aim was to make Sicily the prime kingdom of the known world, and that included the Papal States. In his absence, his subjects had become unruly, and he put down revolts by petty lords with a firm hand. It could not have been the most peaceful place for Anthony to find himself in, but Sicilians remember his stay with great affection, crediting him with divining a well, digging it with his own hands, and planting a lemon tree.

This was a time of trial for the Church. The Crusades had not only lost their original fervour; they had created divisions between those who went and the stay-at-homes who took advantage of the situation by exploiting their lands, upsetting the whole structure of feudalism. From the Emperor to the lowliest peasant, they had to reassess their relationships, and they did not relish the uncertainty of their position. The Mendicant Orders founded by Francis and Dominic did much to renew the spirit of adventure in religion, and everywhere the landscape was being transformed by the intricate beauty of Gothic cathedrals. On the other hand there were strong laymen who were none too scrupulous and sold benefices to the highest bidder. Some minor clergy had to take on servile work to supplement the wretched livings offered by their superiors; there was widespread nepotism, and militant clerics took up arms in the wars between cities and states. Then as now, superstition flourished and astrologers abounded; in spite of a thousand years of Christianity, pagan practices were carried on under cover of legitimate devotions. The devil had a vivid personal reality, and heresy was sweeping like wildfire through France and Italy.

But as on other occasions when the gates of hell threatened the Church of Christ, men were found to come to her aid. They were Francis of Assisi, founder of the Friars Minor, and Dominic of Osma, whose Order of Preachers had its Rule approved in 1216 by Pope Innocent III. Dominic's friars were mendicants, but they were learned men who sought to convert heretics by reasoned argument. Like Anthony, an Iberian, Dominic too had begun his religious life as a Canon Regular, and he adopted the Rule of St Augustine for his black-clad followers, with some additions suitable for their special work. They were well-established in the university towns of Bologna, Oxford and Paris. When Dominic met Francis in Rome, they had

had an instant rapport, in spite of Francis's distrust of academics.

He had said: 'My brothers, my brothers, God has called me by the way of simplicity, and shown me the way of simplicity. I do not want you to name any Rule to me, not St Augustine's, nor St Bernard's, or St Benedict's. The Lord said to me that he wished I should be a new-born simpleton in the world.'

Francis's words echoed St Paul's, about God's foolishness being wiser than human wisdom. Innocent III was too wise to take on two such saints at once, and after this any attempt to amalgamate the two Orders was abandoned.

To combat the current situation, a General Chapter of the Friars Minor was called for Pentecost, 1221. Anthony, barely recovered from his illness, followed his Sicilian friends on the long walk through Italy, to join them at Assisi.

Eventually they saw the outline of Monte Subasio, with the great castle of Rocco at the top, where Francis as a youth had fought amongst the people of the town, to free it from the tyranny of the Duke of Spoleto. The plain from which the Dukedom took its name was spread out before them, and as they drew near to Assisi, they could distinguish the little Chapel of the Portiuncula that Francis loved so particularly because he had repaired it – one of the first works to which he had been called. Here he had received Clare as the first of the poor Ladies; here he had founded his Rule of Poverty upon the account of Jesus sending out his disciples, in the tenth chapter of St Luke. The first glimpse of the cradle of the Order must always be a moving sight for any Franciscan, and Anthony can have been no exception.

Chapters were not only meetings of old acquaintances, and for the reception of new brothers, but legislative assemblies. This one had been called by Peter of Catania, who had become Minister General of the Order the year before, when Francis felt that he could no longer undertake the office. He remained its only true inspiration, but the time had come for another kind of leader. However, Brother Peter died suddenly in mid-Lent, and Elias – a determined, learned man, very ambitious for the Order – was hurried into his place.

All Winter and Spring, Francis had little respite from the illness which was, like Anthony's, the legacy of a Crusade to the Middle East, but when he could, he worked on his new version of the primitive Rule of 1210. He acknowledged that what had been adequate for twelve men from the environs of Assisi might not be appropriate for the three thousand who gathered there on this occasion from all over the known world. They were accommodated in lines of huts made of rush mats with a network of stakes, which they had built with the help of the people of Assisi. The ragged company moved between them, greeting old friends, waiting for the stragglers to come in before starting the discussion of the Rule – the elections to be held to the various offices, and future work apportioned. Anthony would have behaved with diffidence as a very new brother; one moreover who had failed in his first mission. In that great crowd, he must have felt very much alone.

On 23rd May, the feast of Pentecost, the Chapter began. The overwhelming question was, would Francis be well enough to attend? Elias showed every sign of being a strong Minister, but the body cannot function without a heart, and Francis was the heart. A solemn High Mass was celebrated in the open air. The Deacon, a small, dark man, frail and half blind but with a sweet, resonant voice, sang the gospel. A sigh like the wind over a cornfield spread through the ranks of the brothers, and Anthony realised that he was in the presence of his father in Christ at last.

The making of a hermit

After a short period of meditation, the brothers sat down on the grass and listened to Francis's homily. He announced that he would preach on 'Blessed be the Lord, my God, who teacheth my arms to fight.'

Each one of them knew that there was disagreement between those who wished to set up houses that would be owned by the Order, called the Conventuals, and the Friars of the Strict Observance, who clung to the romantic idea of being knights of Lady Poverty. Francis was faithful to her, but it was by no means certain that Elias of Cortina was of the same mind. It seemed that Francis would defend the old Order; his text indicated that it would be a fighting speech, and they waited for the epithets to fly.

But everything Francis did had love as its origin. He addressed the multitude as 'my children', and reminded them that they had promised great things to God, but on His side, He had promised even greater things. Now was the time to perform what they had promised, and look forward with confidence to what God would give them. He warned them that the pleasures of the world were short-lived, and eternity was long; that the pain experienced in this life passed in a moment, but the joys of the next life were inexhaustible. Once again he spoke movingly of the love of Poverty, who was their Lady, and the Church, who was their mother. He urged them to love their brothers, and the entire creation; to have patience in adversity and temperance in prosperity. He ended with a call, by the obedience they had vowed, not to care about what they ate or drank, or worry about material needs, but attend to the one object of praising God in prayer, laying their anxieties on Him who loved them tenderly.

43

Anthony must have remembered this sermon later, when the reformed Rule was discussed – or rather, the embellishment of the old Rule. Francis had dictated it during the intervals between bouts of fever, digestive trouble, and a disease of the eyes which gave him a perpetual headache. It was not a very coherent document; no-one seems to have read it over to him, and with twenty-four chapters it took an inordinate amount of time to process. But to a brother who knew very little of Francis's teaching, it was new and inspirational.

It brought home to Anthony that he really belonged to the Friars Minor, the lesser brothers – that the men around him with their weather-beaten faces and emaciated bodies were his real family. At first they had been an anonymous crowd, but as the debate had gone on, personalities gradually emerged – some impetuous, some cautious. For the nine days that the debate lasted, he received an education in what being a Franciscan really meant. The lessons concerned living a life governed by the Gospels; Francis had made over a hundred references to them. Not that he put any store by books – he once gave the only copy of the New Testament the friars had to a poor woman, knowing it could be sold for a great sum of money.

It emerged that the Rule would forbid the ownership of books; not only because they represented a valuable commodity, but because learning encouraged pride. Francis had many learned men among his friends, but he did not honour them because of their scholarship. He treated them as he treated everyone, with courtesy and affection, but he would rather they did not parade their knowledge. He advocated that clerics who came into the Order should give up their learning, so that they could come naked and innocent to the arms of their crucified Lord.

'Learning takes from many people their docility,' he said, 'and does not permit them to bend to humble practices.'

He asked the educated man to live in a place removed from the noise of the world, where he could think over his

44

life in sorrow; to have his heart changed by tranquil recollection and aspire to better things. Francis considered that the kind of man who could do this would be ready to go back into the world like a lion refreshed, his thirst for the word satisfied by the water of the spirit; and he explained: 'He may then be assigned confidently to the true ministry of the word, for he will pour out what is bubbling up within him.'

He urged the brothers not to seek learning at the expense of virtue, especially if it threatened their vocation. If trials came, books which were not useful should be jettisoned. He hated volumes of philosophy that made rhetorical points, or analysed ideas out of existence. The old chronicler, Thomas of Celano, said that to a lay brother who wanted a Psalter, he had given some ashes. Franciscan lay brothers were meant to pray the 'Our Father' as Christ had taught them. Only the priests were allowed a breviary, so that they could say the Divine Office. Repetitive prayer has its place in many religions, and Francis was ahead of his time in advocating it. He made no allowance for its tedium, only seeing that it could soothe the harsh clamour of intellectual striving, and lead the way to peace.

This might well have alienated Anthony, for his learning was the only thing he had left. The story of the Pro-Martyrs had moved him to offer his life for the Faith, but God had rejected his offer. He had spent ten years of that life amongst books, whose authors had become friends and guides; his mind was saturated in learning. How could he ever emulate Francis's ideal of a simple friar, ready to sacrifice his mind for Christ? Surely martyrdom would have seemed easier.

Anthony must have been tempted to ignore the food brought as their contribution to the assembly by the people of Assisi. The brothers ate at twenty-three long trestle-tables and were more used to scraps than the magnificent capons and wines of Umbria which they were offered, but they were bound by the laws of courtesy to accept everything; after one General Chapter, they had been obliged to stay an extra two days in order to finish up what was left over. In this they followed Francis himself; though the servant of all, he had the manners of a prince.

But there was more to being a friar than kissing lepers and giving one's tunic to the poor; in any case, most of their tunics were so worn and patched, they would have had an unenthusiastic reception from any but the most destitute. An heroic degree of tolerance had to be exercised among the brothers. It was easy to be patient with a stranger for a limited time; much more difficult to be equally well-disposed toward the brother you lived with, day in and day out. Francis called on them to 'exchange chaste embraces, gentle feelings, holy kisses, pleasing conversation, modest laughter, and joyous looks'. The mark of the Order was the holy joy and brotherly love which were part of Francis's character. They were there in the French songs he sang when he was particularly happy – and that could be the result of a humiliation or a temptation overcome, as much as by an overwhelming feeling of thanks for the gift of creation.

Owning nothing, the brothers did not have to suffer anxiety about losing anything. If they felt pain at having to part with an especially loved friend, they offered it up to the Saviour who had been abandoned at the time of his greatest need. And because he had not withheld friendship from Judas who had betrayed him, they must love their enemies too.

This last injunction Francis probably took to himself, well aware that some of the brothers thought that he was holding the Order back from its true destiny as the saviour of the Church. He did not love the would-be reformers any less, but at the same time he regarded them as traitors. He could forgive the criticism of himself; there had been times in the past when he had put a brother under obedience to deride him, and gloried in the resulting diatribe. But those who betrayed Lady Poverty by being unfaithful to her were not to be trusted – yet he accepted that Elias was now his superior and he must obey him.

As the days went by, Anthony saw Francis growing weaker. His voice, which had once been clear and full, had faded to a whisper. He sat at Elias's feet, and when he wished to be heard, he plucked at Elias's habit to draw attention to what he had to say. Around him the arguments of the Conventuals and friars of the Strict Observance eddied and flowed; it seemed that his wishes were being ignored. Anthony must have wondered how many men could have abdicated their authority to someone else, and put the future of the Order in other hands.

There were lessons to be learned from this moving humility. Above all, Francis's plight appealed to a very deep emotion in Anthony – his pity. That would be more and more in evidence as he grew in the religious life, and is the source of many of the wonders ascribed to him. Now it made him resolve to leave his own future in the hands of God. For himself, he would seek nothing but Christ, and Christ crucified.

As the discussion of the Rule neared its end, they reached a passage in which Francis had attempted to put into words an idea which perhaps only music could express. It was a declaration of love and praise for a Being unknowable, unfathomable, yet to be desired for all eternity. He was trying to do something that a collection of nouns and adjectives could barely hint at, yet as the words were read out many of those listening must have been touched to the heart. Was it then that Anthony decided always to be true to the spirit of the Founder, because no-one was more faithful?

Francis had seemed contradictory about the way in which friars should react to authority; on the one hand he said that nobody should obey a superior if it offended his conscience – which it was feared would lead to anarchy – yet at the same time perfect obedience entailed anticipating the wishes of the superior, and obeying them before they were voiced, which demanded a degree of intimacy between them which was being lost as the Order grew. Ever afterwards, Anthony tried to achieve this in his dealings with his superiors.

Then someone stepped forward to tell those who had not already heard it what was known of the death of the martyrs in Morocco. After this, Francis was moved to say: 'Now indeed I can say that I possess five true friars.' The news was received with joy, but Francis detected a note of self-congratulation in it; and perhaps it offended against true humility. At any event he silenced it with: 'Let every brother exult in his own martyrdom, not that of others.'

The Rule of 1221 was never formally rejected, but it was unworkable, and everyone knew it – including Francis himself. When the next revision was made two years later, it was imposed by others without reference to him. This left him free to become a hermit, something he had longed to do; only advice from Sister Clare, who felt that he still had much to offer the Order, had prevented him from doing it long ago. Before him lay identification with Christ – the final gift – the stigmata.

But there was something left for him to initiate in the Chapter. There had been a disastrous mission to Germany in 1219 by some sixty friars, who between them spoke only one word of the language, and that was 'Ja'. They had resolved in truly Franciscan fashion to say 'Ja' to everything; when they were asked if they belonged to the heretical sect, the Cathars, they replied with the same affirmative. Some of them were beaten and some exhibited at a fair; these humiliations may have delighted them, but they gained no converts. Dominic's Friar Preachers had been more successful, and there may have been an element of competition in the evangelisation; at any rate Francis decided to make another attempt. So that the previous reception would not be repeated, he called for German-speaking volunteers only.

Eighty friars leaped to their feet and were put under the command of Caesar of Spires, a loyal friend of Francis. Anthony, not being a German speaker, was debarred from joining the expedition, which might well have restored his shattered confidence. Singly and in groups the friars were allocated their next assignments. In the words of an early legend: 'No minister sought for Anthony, because he was known of none.' It was obvious, as the brothers hurried on their way like a colony of brown ants going purposefully about their business, that he must make a move on his own.

Nearby was a man with an air of authority, whom he learned was Brother Gratian, the Provincial of Romagna. How he would receive a request from an unknown friar with only a failed mission behind him was open to question; somehow Anthony found the courage to beg him for a position of some kind – any kind – within his Province. He did not mention that he had studied with the Canons Regular for ten years; that was all behind him now. He knew what was expected of a Franciscan friar, and the most menial task would be his greatest pleasure. One thing he requested – work that would 'form him in the practise of religious discipline'.

Possibly Anthony had used Latin to eke out his newly-acquired Italian – or Gratian may have noticed that he had a breviary – but something made him ask if he were a priest. On hearing that he was, he told him that a group of lay brothers at Monte Paolo, near Forlì in Romagna, had asked for a priest to say mass for them. Apart from exercising his priestly office, he could also make himself useful in the convent.

When they reached the mountain from which the hermitage took its name, Anthony knew that he was fulfilling his destiny. It was quiet and remote, a suitable place for contemplation. Like St Anthony of Egypt, whose name he had taken, he could live the life of a hermit. He and Brother Gratian climbed four hundred feet, and through the mist they had a view across the plain of the Romagna to the distant Adriatic. They may well have said Francis's prayer on reaching a new place: 'O Christ, we bless thee here and in all thy churches the world over, because by thy holy cross thou hast redeemed the world.'

The 'church' at Monte Paolo was probably a chapel, hardly bigger than the huts in which the brothers lived. To add to the penances they inflicted upon themselves, it was searingly hot in summer and near freezing in winter.

Francis wished all his friars to have some experience of the contemplative life; he was always afraid that their missionary labours, the long walks between villages, towns and cities, and the gathering of alms, would absorb too much time that belonged to God. As he put it: 'Let those friars, to whom the Lord has given the grace of working, work faithfully and with devotion; in such wise however that while keeping aloof from idleness, the enemy of the soul, they take care not to extinguish the spirit of prayer and devotion to which all temporal things should be subservient.' He also added to the Rule, a copy of which the friars were encouraged to carry beneath their patched tunics, a direction for the conduct of hermitages.

He wished the number of brothers to be kept small. The community that Anthony found at Monte Paolo was considered adequate at just six, divided into two sets of three. Francis, with his feeling for the family, called one set 'mothers' and the other 'sons'. It is interesting that he had a very special feeling for mothers and the work they did, perhaps because his own mother had done her best to protect him from his father's wrath in the early days of his conversion. When he was apportioning personality to the elements in creation that surrounded him, all the gentler, softer things were his sisters, including one he had longed for – Sister Death, in the form of martyrdom.

Francis adapted his Rule from the practice of a Spanish community, who changed their roles every week, though he may have thought this might unsettling or too restrictive, because he left the amount of time flexible. The Mothers were cast in the role of Martha, who was distracted with much serving, the archetype of all those trapped in household tasks that have to be done. The Sons were Mary, sitting at Jesus's feet, drinking in his words and overcome with love. Francis evidently thought these roles were interchangeable and not decided by gender, and today we are coming round to his way of thinking.

The brothers lived inside an enclosure; each had his own cell for sleeping and for contemplation. They gathered together for the Offices of the Church as they would have done in a more traditional monastery, and kept silence between Compline and Tierce. They also ate together; the Mothers were responsible for obtaining the food, either from the bounty of nature or by begging. This must have taken up a great deal of their time, as the nearest habitation was Forlì, about three miles away, and they would have had to travel even further afield when they had worn out their welcome there. Unwelcome visitors who might disturb the Sons' contemplation were dismissed by the Mothers.

When Anthony was a Mother he was expected to wash dishes and scrub floors like the rest, and tradition has it that he performed these routine tasks very cheerfully. As a priest, he had no special privileges, though one of the brothers gave him the use of a grotto or cave, rather removed from the others and probably damp and cold. We gather from some of the chroniclers that he added to its natural disadvantages by making a slice of bread and a little water his sole nourishment for the day.

There was nothing tranquil or soft about his contemplations. He subjected himself to strenuous penances in order to subdue his body from desires, not evil in themselves, but impeding his progress in the spiritual life. And he seems to have been tempted by the devil. This might be dismissed as an hallucination brought on by a starvation diet, but it is not only the mediaeval mind that can believe in the embodiment of evil. What is it that disturbs our attempts at prayer with trivial and random thoughts, or, when God seems near, tries to prise us apart? There is evidence of a malevolent presence in every news bulletin; if we believe in a personal God, we cannot rule out that his enemies are personal too. Very holy people have had experience of this threat to their peace of mind, telling us that it can only be dismissed by prayer and fasting, and Anthony was no exception.

We are told that his austerities deprived him of sleep, and he was often too exhausted to drag himself from his secluded cell to join the brothers in the Divine Office. We are told that his desire to do so was so strong that he accepted their help into the chapel, though this account may be suspect, since it is also mentioned that he always answered the bell that called them to their evening meal. He certainly seems to have done his best to be treated exactly like all the others; it never occurred to them that he was possessed of any great learning, or had lived a life of luxury in the world. A rejection of their past lives and absolute equality was demanded of all Franciscans, and Anthony observed this injunction scrupulously.

The Chapel that stands today in the woods at Monte Paolo is said to have been built with stones from the old friary, but it is not likely that it was constructed of such durable material, unless the friars had taken over the use of an existing building. They would not, of course, have been allowed to own it. Anthony seems to have shared the life of the lay brothers for about a year, when an event took place that was to elevate him to another sphere altogether.

It happened at an ordination ceremony at Forlì, to which the brothers had been invited. From subsequent events it seems that this was well-attended, and by influential clerics, perhaps from the nearby university city of Bologna. A number of Friars Minor were present, together with some from the Order of Preachers, and it was from these that the candidates for ordination were drawn. To accommodate such a number, it is likely that the event took place in the Cathedral, performed by the Bishop; the Franciscan Minister Provincial, Brother Gratian would have been present. Forlì was of some importance due to its proximity to the Roman road, the Via Emilia, which was still used as a main highway to the coast.

After the ceremony there must have been a celebratory meal for the new priests and other guests, and the question arose – who should address the assembly? This was evidently not part of the formal proceedings, and no-one had been appointed to speak; certainly no-one volunteered. The Dominicans who were approached pleaded lack of time for preparation, an excuse that would scarcely have held water, as their Order had been founded to preach in season and out, to refute heresy and comfort the faithful, so perhaps they had dined too well.

Then Brother Gratian caught sight of Anthony. He must have heard him speak several times since he had been in the Province, and remembered that his Latin was witty and elegant. As the circumstances were informal, the content of the address was not important, and in the event of a failure to interest or elevate the assembly, he could always excuse Anthony of the grounds of his inexperience.

At first Anthony demurred, but Brother Gratian insisted on obedience, and he rose to his feet, no doubt sending up a desperate prayer for support in this unexpected situation. Inspiration came to him, and he announced a text from St Paul's letter to the Philippines: 'He humbled himself and became obedient unto death, even death on a cross.'

For a while, we are told, nervousness made him ill-at-ease, for he was a novice preacher, addressing many who were practised in the art. It was two years since he had used his books, and he would have had to search the recesses of his mind for suitable quotations from the scriptures. But if the last year had taught him anything, it was that simple faith had its own message; what he lacked in polish he could make up in fervour. He plunged into his discourse, and the dammed-up eloquence of the years he had spent as a friar poured forth; the heartfelt prayer bore fruit.

There were nods of approval as he elaborated on his theme; his freshness and enthusiasm touched his hearers as he spoke of the sublime humility of Jesus. By the time he finished speaking, they knew they were in the presence of a preacher of genius.

This had far-reaching consequences, both for him and the Order to which he belonged. Those in authority were exercised about the growth of the Cathari in Italy and the Albigensians in France. These were the inheritors of the Manicheism of the Fourth Century, which had once claimed Anthony's hero St Augustine among its followers. He had

53

escaped their clutches, and fought them all the more successfully because he was well-acquainted with their arguments.

These heretics believed that there were two principles, Good and Evil, which were the twin creators of all that existed; the Good created the invisible world, and the Evil the visible world. This made life a nightmare where the body and all that sustained it was vile. Absolutists in the sect held that Good and Evil were equal in strength; the less severe believed that evil was inferior and owed its creation to the good. Catholics, of course, could not countenance the idea that anything evil could come from God. The question of evil in the world has always been the great religious problem. It persists into our own day, though because of the decline of faith it is less tenaciously argued, but in the Thirteenth Century it was a matter of life and death.

The Cathari and the Albigensians had taken advantage of the laxness of secular priests, and the worldliness of the religious orders, to claim that their hierarchy was more genuinely holy. At the height of their popularity they had their own Bishops, but lay people also had a place in their rituals. Many attended the Catholic sacraments, preached austerities, and had a name for sanctity. Frederick II, who had recently been crowned Emperor at Rome, saw in this freethinking movement a threat to his own power, and successive Popes declared war upon it, but foot-soldiers were needed to fight the battle.

As far back as 1203, when Dominic was a Canon Regular of St Augustine, he and the Bishop of Osma had been travelling through the South of France on a diplomatic mission for Alphonse IX, the King of Castile, and they were shocked by the inroads made by the heretics. Passing through Toulouse, they were entertained by a man Dominic discovered belonged to the Cathari, and he spent all his energies on a dialogue to convert him, without any apparent success – until, overnight, he found that divine grace had given their host a Damascus experience. This personal encounter revealed his vocation, and he resolved to root out heresy, founding his Order of Preachers to do missionary work wherever it was needed. By 1215 the dream had become a reality, with papal approval, but in 1221, soon after his meeting with Francis, Dominic died, and though there were many able preachers in the Order, he left a gap that could not easily be filled.

We do not have names for the individuals who saw in Anthony a successor to the great warrior against the heretics, but someone recognised the potential in this dark young man with a voice that could ring out richly and strike a chord in his hearers. He was gifted with a personality of charm and sweetness, and he would have been surrounded by an admiring circle of people ready to congratulate him, realising that his erudition was matched by his humility. His courage in meeting the challenge argued strength of character, and he was scholarly enough to meet the most well-read heretic on his own ground and outdo him in argument. It was decided to groom him for his new apostolate.

There was something else in his favour. Dominic had become associated with Simon de Montfort's crusade against the Albigensians, which had been conducted with great cruelty. It was effective, but the Dominican Order was tarnished by implication, and though Dominic himself had never been responsible for the death sentence of a single heretic, it left many Christians uneasy. Anthony had no such disadvantage. His attitude was:

'One does not set fire to a house where a corpse reposes. You should not burn the temple from which God has been ejected by the sin of heresy, especially if there is any hope of conversion. And even if you are certain that obstinacy will continue, there is still room for patience, for God Himself is the first to give us example. I repeat – have patience.'

It was with this conviction that he began to prepare for his great mission. Some authorities think that he spent some time with Thomas Gallo, a distinguished professor who had studied in Paris and was the translator from the Greek of the works of Denis the Areopagite. He was Abbot of the monastery of St Andrew in Vercelli, and the journey would have been straightforward; up the Appenine range and across the rice paddy-fields of Piedmonte. Whether the relationship was that of master and pupil, or friend and colleague, is not clear. There is the suggestion of an end-of-term report about the beginning of Gallo's assessment of the young Anthony: 'Although he was not learned in the natural sciences, he was truly holy and easily understood mystical theology' – but he went on to say: 'Like John the Baptist, he was a lamp burning and shining. Because his heart was burning with the love of God, he too was a shining example to men.'

It was with these credentials that Anthony set out to begin the work that would occupy him for the rest of his life.

The making of a preacher

Anthony's first assignment was to preach in the Province of Romagna, which then comprised the whole of Lombardy, including the valley of the Po, with its mouth on the Adriatic, and the lakes and mountains in the north. Amphitheatres which had existed since Roman times were plundered for stones to construct the great Gothic churches then being built everywhere, surrounded by the elegant town houses of the rich and the hovels of the poor. Most of the larger towns grew up from Roman way-stations on the Via Emilia, still much used, since it was on the pilgrimage route to Rome. Anthony would have been familiar with Modena and its Romanesque Duomo, with lions crouching by the west door, and Bologna with its university and hundreds of towers, giving the skyline its distinctive character.

Where the friars were established he stayed with them, or used the hospices of monasteries, though he sometimes slept on the bare ground with a stone for his pillow. An early biographer assures us: 'His zeal for souls gave him no rest.' He must, if he travelled towards the coast from Forlì, have reached the town of Rimini, the place where the Cathari were most entrenched. It had been in the hands of the Papacy since the Eighth Century, but by Anthony's time its hold was precarious. Two years before he arrived, St Aldobrand, the Bishop of Fossombrone, had attempted to preach a mission there but had been roughly handled by the heretics and was hard put to it to escape with his life.

Unlike the Bishop, Anthony did not come with an entourage. Accompanied only by his socius, he lived an example of poverty and simplicity, rivalling the austerity of the Cathari themselves. Even so, although he was not physically attacked, no-one took much notice of this small, dark man with a foreign accent. As a seaport, the town was full of strangers; one more or less was not a novelty. Anthony must have racked his brains to think of some way to attract their attention.

One day he was walking by the clear waters of the river on its way to the sea, and he stood on a bank between the two bodies of water. There were fish swimming close to the bank, and in his great disappointment at failing to get any other hearers, he addressed them as if they were a human crowd. The writer of the Fioretti tells us that he said: 'Hear the word of God, O ye fishes of the sea and of the river, since the infidel heretics refuse to hear it.' And apparently a great shoal of fish appeared, larger than had been seen in that place before, holding their heads out of the water, all facing Anthony. They were assembled in order of size, the small ones nearest the bank, the middle-sized ones behind them, and the largest fish out in deeper water. Since they seemed to be listening, Anthony appealed to them to give thanks to God for their creation, because the element they lived in was clean and wholesome and provided food for their nourishment. God had given them the command to increase and multiply, and blessed them as they continued to do so. When the Flood came and all the land-based animals were overwhelmed, they were kept free from harm. To them had been given the stewardship of the prophet Jonah, and they had disgorged him on to dry land after three days.

Anthony remembered too the miracle by which St Peter was sent to catch the fish with a coin in its mouth, to pay the tribute for Jesus, who was so poor that he lacked the necessary money. They provided food for the Lord both before his Resurrection and also afterwards, in a mysterious fashion not given to man to understand. He said that for all these things they must praise and bless God who had given them greater blessings than to any other creatures.

The account goes on in these words: 'The fishes began to open their mouths and bow their heads and show other marks of reverence. Anthony was so much encouraged by this, and the appearance of yet more fish, that he cried out: "Blessed be God eternal, since the fishes of the waters give Him more honour than do the heretics, and the animals that have no reason pay more heed to His word than unbelieving man.'"

We are told that as the sermon progressed, none of the fish swam away, but remained attentive until the end. People passing by noticed the great shoal of fish listening to the ragged friar's harangue, and were at first moved by curiosity, then won over by his strange power, and listened to him in their turn.

Taking full advantage of this opportunity, he outlined the truths of the Catholic faith, and many came to see the errors of the Cathari. When Anthony finished his discourse, he sent the fishes on their way with a blessing and they departed, 'showing marvellous signs of joy' – though the Fioretti does not explain what these were. Artists have found the story irresistible as a subject, and it has been represented in many media through subsequent centuries.

From then on, Anthony's mission began to prosper. He made a prolonged stay in Rimini, inviting prominent members of the Cathari to state their case and explain the difficulties they experienced in coming to terms with Catholic doctrine. Like Francis, he was always courteous, and this impressed them more than any show of anger would have done. There were some remarkable conversions, and in one case a man called Bonillo, who for thirty years had been an inveterate heretic, was completely won over, and led the way for one of his servants to become a Franciscan. This man was notable for his devotion, and he was beatified under the name of John Baronci. Not everyone responded so readily, but at least the gullible were less likely to listen to Cathari propaganda, and many who were tempted to do so resisted it.

Anthony did encounter some active resistance, and this was dramatically shown in the story of the heretics who invited him to dine. In imitation of Jesus, who ate with both sinners and the Pharisees in order to recover their souls for God, Anthony accepted the invitation – but the heretics had resolved to get rid of him by giving him poisoned food. Whether there was something amiss with the dish he was offered, or as the legend has it, he received a premonition, divinely inspired, he reproached his host for his evil intention. The man was evidently quick-witted, and said he had only added poison to prove Christ's promise that his true disciple would be able to take any poisonous thing without coming to harm. Making the sign of the cross over the dish, Anthony began to eat with as much appetite as he could muster in the circumstances. As the hours went by without his showing any symptoms of poisoning, the threat of death receded, much to his relief and the frustration of his enemies. Word of his escape soon got about, which was widely regarded as miraculous, and as a result he was assured of a ready audience for his sermons.

In his imitation of Christ, he became more and more like Francis himself. Although they were temperamentally very different, Francis being full of spontaneous energy and Anthony more shy – and of course one of the intellectuals of whom Francis was so wary – they also had much in common. They both had personalities which could win over listeners as they went about as itinerant preachers, and they both relied on the word of God as demonstrated in the Scriptures. Anthony had preached to the fishes as Francis had preached to the birds, because both men were filled with love for creation and wanted all things to share in their exaltation. All Francis's brothers revered him, but Anthony had a special desire to model himself upon him. In the next year, after his long spell of preaching in Romagna, he is thought to have been in a position to observe Francis more closely.

In 1223 there was a Whitsun Chapter at Assisi, presided over by Ugolino, Cardinal Bishop of Ostia, the chief protector and corrector of the Franciscan Order. During the Chapter a new Rule was presented to the assembled friars, compiled by Ugolino, and this incorporated hardly any of

Francis's own ideas. It was a complete triumph for Brother Elias, who was acting as Minister General and had actually repressed one of Francis's drafts, claiming that it had been lost. He considered himself obliged to do this because the Order of Friars Minor had grown unmanageable. There was a rift between those who wanted to preserve Francis's original inspiration, and those who felt the time for that had passed forever. The new men had their way, and Francis, to whom obedience was sovereign, acquiesced. He agreed to go to Rome and be present when the Rule was offered to Pope Honorius for approval.

Salimibene, a very early Franciscan writer who joined the Order only seven years after Anthony's death, calls him Francis's socius, and must have meant that in its Franciscan sense. The word was used in the Order to denote a travelling companion, and the office dated back, as so much of Francis's teaching did, to the early disciples, who were sent out two by two on their work of evangelisation. Each acted as the servant, helper, and when necessary amanuensis of the other. If Anthony did serve as Francis's companion, it is most likely that he did so on this journey to Rome. After it, Francis retired into contemplation, offering himself up to imitation of the suffering of Christ, while Anthony was travelling in France and Italy on active missions. His success so far would have qualified him for inclusion on the journey; if Ugolino had met him during the Chapter, he would have approved of his intellectual capacity, and appreciated his personal devotion to Francis.

It is not recorded what happened between Francis and Anthony. Perhaps Anthony managed to persuade Francis that it was not such a bad thing if books were allowed to be used, because the Rule of 1223 did permit their ownership. One thing is certain; they parted on good terms, because there exists a letter which caught up with Anthony when he was in Bologna, reading –

'To his dearest Brother Anthony, Brother Francis wishes health. It is my desire that you should teach the brothers sacred theology, on condition that neither in you or in them, the spirit of holy prayer, conformable to the Rule we profess, be quenched. God speed you.'

And it was addressed to 'Anthony, my Bishop'. Francis had given him a final accolade – a nickname – in the same spirit that he called Cardinal Ugolino 'My Pope'.

In the light of this authentic document, we cannot doubt the special place each occupied in the other's heart, and the warmth of that greeting is unmistakable. Knowing what we do of both men, is there perhaps a hint that many discussions on the subject of theological studies, advocated by Anthony and objected to strenuously by Francis, had taken place? Certainly Francis made a complete abdication of his former prejudice, but added a loving injunction to Anthony, not to become so immersed in study as to lose sight of the pursuit of holiness. But Francis no longer believed the two courses were incompatible, and it must have been Anthony who brought about this revolution in his thinking. The permission was given to someone he knew and trusted, not a stranger, however well recommended. And he refers to the Rule, determined to conform to what bound the whole Order together; a subject they had talked of, over and over again. To call Anthony 'my Bishop' was also an act of humility, very typical of Francis.

No doubt Anthony set to work at once in the university city; we know that the Franciscans of Bologna had a school attached to their convent, and this must have been the first of his foundations. No record survives of the impression he left as a teacher, and perhaps it was as an organiser that he excelled, since we shall see that he later became the successful administrator of a Province. But there are numerous accounts of him as a preacher, and some of his sermons have come down to us, though mostly in the form of notes. These he left as a heritage to further generations of preachers. As a theologian he occupied the ground between the Desert Fathers and later giants like St Bonaventure, who joined the Friars Minor only ten years after Anthony's death and benefited from the theological institutes he founded, elaborating Anthony's ideas about such doctrines as transubstantiation and his ~~█████████~~ Marian devotion.

The sermons of Anthony are contained in the Antonian Library at Padua. Of particular note is the Codex Del Tesoro, which is of great antiquity and was once kept in the Basilica; wrapped in silk and placed in a crystal case, it was carried in procession on suitable feasts. It was popularly believed to be a missal or a Bible annotated by him, but when opened in the Nineteenth Century it was found to contain a copy of his sermons, and this was subsequently used by scholars to validate his works.

He had a high regard for his calling, leaving a description of preachers as 'weightless clouds, liberated from the onerous attachment to temporal things. Their words fall from their mouths like rain; at times they boom with threats like peals of thunder. The good examples of their holy lives shine forth like flashes of lightning.'

We are reminded by this that he was called 'The Hammer of the Heretics' and also that he never lost sight of Francis's call to prayer before everything. It was not enough merely to proclaim the Gospel; he lived it. He also insisted that the good preacher must be the source of life and faith; as the sun is the source of light and heat, the preacher should be equally clear and heart-warming in his teaching.

His method may fairly be said to be based on using the Gospel, Epistle and Introit of the day, and the scriptural lessons of the Divine Office, which was something of an innovation. Over and over again his voice is described as a clarion call; one chronicler said his name meant 'Alte tonens' – 'he who thunders with great force'. It was his habit to look over the heads of a crowd, projecting his discourse to the furthest of his hearers. He aimed at the simplest language, without resort to sarcasm, abuse or ornate words that showed off his learning. Occasionally he could, appealingly enough, be carried away by his own eloquence. One bemused listener tells us of his speaking to some religious, when 'his divine wisdom was hidden in mystery, and he uttered thoughts so beautiful and so profound concerning the scriptures, that few of his auditors could fully understand the beauty of his exposition, even those among them who had long practice in seeking to understand texts.'

Usually he aimed at moving his audience to sorrow for sin, true contrition, and a resolution to amend their lives. He was extraordinarily successful in this, and later in his career had to keep a number of confessors on hand to cope with the demand for their services. He tried to inspire hope and offer help, and while absolutely sincere, he did not despise the qualities of charm and tact in gaining the affection of the crowds.

But he could be as blunt and direct with the wealthy and influential as Jesus was with the Pharisees. We do not know the place or occasion, but he is reported to have corrected the well-to-do with a full measure of frankness when he considered it his duty. The old recorder says he 'pierced them with the javelin of plain speech'. So great was his courage in not being intimidated by power and authority, that other preachers who were present 'trembled at his temerity and, filled with shame and confusion, hid their glowing faces in their handkerchiefs or their sleeves, and wished they were anywhere else, rather than where they were.' There is no instance in which he was subjected to violence because of his plain speaking. The worst he had to deal with was indifference, and that only in the early days of his apostolate, perhaps before he learned from experience how to play on the feelings of those who gathered to listen to him.

Some of these may only have needed reminding of the scriptures they were already grounded in, but he seems to have succeeded in making them aware of a new way to apply them to their lives. Those who had never heard them before – and this would include the great majority – must have felt much in common with the disciples of the early Church, listening to the Apostles when the Gospels were literally the Good News. This was something he must have learned from Francis, whose words were the clear reflection of Jesus's own teaching.

Anthony was also in debt to St Augustine, both for his rhetoric and for the formation of his thought. The difference between them can perhaps best be illustrated by their approach to the subject of humility. St Augustine writes: 'Our perfection may be compared to a magnificent temple, which we must raise in the soul for the Lord to dwell therein. And if you ask me what should be the first and fundamental layer of this mystic edifice, I answer – humility. Humility is the root of every virtue, as pride is the root of every vice.'

Anthony says: 'Consider the earthworm; he contracts himself in order that he may be better able to extend, and thus the soul must retire into itself by humility in order the better to raise itself to heavenly things.' There spoke the Franciscan who was bound to walk with downcast eyes, on the advice of his founder. The great advantage of this was that he had a profound appreciation of what happened at his feet. The earthworms Francis rescued from the well-trodden paths were as perfectly suited as analogies for Anthony's audience, as Augustine's noble buildings were for the inhabitants of Roman North Africa.

He followed St Augustine in using symbols from the natural world – flowers, rainbows, dawn and sunset, storms, blossom and fruit all serve as images of the spiritual life. One elaborate passage reads: 'There is a threefold evening and a threefold morning; a threefold weeping and a three-fold gladness. The threefold evening is – first, the sad evening of the fall of our first parents in Paradise; second, the sad evening of the bitter Passion and Death of our Redeemer; and third, the sad evening of our own fast-approaching death. The threefold morning is – first, the glad morning of the Birth of the Messiah; second, the glad morning of the Lord's Resurrection; and third, the glad morning of our own future resurrection.' This symmetry and elegance is typical.

When preaching to religious he remembered their special needs. His life as a mendicant friar had taken him far from the cloister but he recalled it as a refuge from the evil of the cities. He visualised the religious soul finding in the Heart of Jesus sanctuary from the wiles and attacks of the devil, and a delightful retreat; and he urged everyone to press on to the very source from which the blood springs in the Divine Heart, promising that there they would find light, peace and consolation.

The religious soul he compared to the dove who makes her nest in the deep hollow of the rock. The nest is made of little pieces of straw which the world despises as useless, but for the religious they are the virtues practised by the Saviour; humility, meekness, poverty, patience and mortification. These, he pointed out, were the material with which to construct a dwelling-place for ever in the deepest hollow of the rock, in the Heart of Jesus. We have seen how Anthony spent days at a time in the cave at Monte Paolo, and it was this he must have been remembering. In the profound silence of prayer, he might well have watched a dove making her nest, and retained the image he used with such a moving effect.

Yet he often drew upon his extensive reading at Coimbra for quotations to embellish his sermons. Amongst all the theologians, St Augustine was his favourite, as we see from a sermon he preached on the Sixth Sunday after Pentecost. It is on the Trinity, and begins with a quotation from St John (15:26).

'But when the Counsellor comes whom I shall send from the Father, even the Spirit of truth who proceeds from the Father, he will bear witness to me.' Anthony asked his listeners to note first of all that the doctrine of the Trinity is openly manifested in this Gospel. 'The Holy Spirit is sent by the Father and the Son; all three are one in substance and inseparably equal; their essence is one, but their persons three. The Lord makes clear the Unity of their Divine essence and the Trinity of their persons when he says in Matthew: "Go and baptise all peoples in the name of the Father, and of the Son, and of the Holy Spirit." He says "in the name" rather than "in the names", to show the unity of their essence, but by using three names he shows that they are three persons.'

'In this Trinity are to be found the supreme origin of all things, the most perfect beauty, and the most blessed delight. As Augustine shows us in his book on the true religion, by the supreme origin of all things we mean God the Father; from Him come both the Son and the Holy Spirit. By the most perfect beauty we mean His Son, who is truly one with the Father, alike to him in all things, whom we venerate with Him and in Him. The Son is the model of all things, since by him all things are made, and to Him they return. By the most blessed delight and the sum of happiness we mean the Holy Spirit, who is the gift of the Father and the Son, and in whose unchangeable equality with them it is our duty to believe.'

'Through contemplation we therefore become conscious that we are the creation of this Unity in the Trinity. We have our being from the Father, through the Son, and in the Holy Spirit. The Father is our beginning, to Whom we return; the Son is the model we follow; and from the Holy Spirit comes the grace by which we are reconciled to them. As we strive to contemplate our Creator, and to believe that He is truly One in Three and Three in One, we see something like a mirror of the Trinity in the human mind itself.'

'This is what Augustine speaks about in his book on the Trinity, when he says that the human mind, the best part of our nature, is where an image of the Trinity may be discovered. The mind is composed of the memory, the understanding, and the will or affection. If we examine these qualities we can discern an image of God's own nature as Trinity. Memory, understanding, and will or affection are a trinity, but together they are one mind, not three; one essence, not three. Memory, understanding, and will or affection each work on things outside themselves, but together they make one life, one mind, one essence. Each of them can be perceived separately, yet together they exist as one mind.'

'The mind is like a parent, whose child is knowledge or understanding. When the mind thinks, it gives birth to understanding, and from these two proceeds love, because the mind loves the thought within itself. Nothing can love itself unless it first understands itself; it is the embrace between this parent (the mind) and the child (the understanding) that generates love. So you see that in the interaction between these three concepts there is a reflection of the Trinity.'

We may well wonder at the reception these complicated ideas received from people who could not read or write, and had only a distant view of the Mass; they came to listen to him because they had heard he was the preacher of the moment, and it was the custom to regard religion as a welcome respite from a hard life; the only rival to it was the musician or story-teller round the fire. There was something about Anthony that held them enthralled, whether they understood him or not. He never talked down to them, and he spoke to each one as if he or she were capable of understanding.

Words had a magic in those days, when language was evolving rapidly. It was about the time when Anthony became a friar that the sonnet form was first developed in Italy. Even the illiterate could appreciate a well-turned cadence; its measured formality was respected – and no-one played with words and their meanings with more zest than Anthony. He went back to their Greek and Latin roots for his images, and would split them into their component syllables – even into vowels and consonants, in order to make a point. He was like a child on the seashore, sorting pebbles, putting them into piles according to their shape or colour, and finally throwing them into the sea to make an almighty splash. The well-educated found in his sermons something for their minds to bite on, and they were equally aware of their artistic quality. But he was not only concerned with philosophical concepts.

In a sermon on the Assumption, he likens the Virgin to an olive and a cypress, both trees that figured in the landscape which surrounded his hearers, as he said: 'The olive tree is a plant, the olive is the fruit, and the oil is the juice. The olive tree gives us first a sweet-smelling flower which later becomes an olive. This is first green, then red, after which it reaches maturity. The blessed Anne was like the olive tree that produced the white flower with a perfume not to be described, that is to say the Holy Mary; and the latter was green, because of the conception and birth of the Son of God.' (The word 'green' is used to describe a virgin.) 'In the conception and birth of the Saviour, the Blessed Virgin kept her virginity and so retained her virtue. She remained virgin both before and after the birth of her son. She partook of the nature of the purple fruit during the Passion of her son, which pierced her very soul. Finally, she reached maturity at her Assumption, which we celebrate today; for she has obtained both power and joy in the glory of the heavenly beatitudes.' The reference to the cypress is more fleeting; Anthony uses it to illustrate that: 'The cypress is above all other trees, as Mary is above the angels in glory as she is honoured in the Feast.'

In this way he ensured that the next time this hearers saw an olive, it would remind them of the Assumption, and continue to do so as they watched the fruit mature in its season. He stamped everything they encountered in their daily lives with the image of the Creator, his mother, his angels and his saints. Later they would carve them on their churches, each artisan truly an artist and a philosopher, and leave these images carved upon the consciousness of succeeding generations.

Anthony may have spoken Latin to refute well-educated heretics when it was important to tackle their errors with the greatest accuracy; or to share his more abstract ideas with university graduates, or members of religious orders. But it is generally accepted that he normally used the vernacular, and he must have perfected both his Italian and his French because we shall see, after this digression into his methods as a preacher, how he used the instrument he had forged to awaken hearts and minds to the beauties of religion.

The mission to France

The Church's battle against the Albigensians had been
going on since the time of Pope Innocent III, who was
elected in 1198. He brought the Papacy to the highest point
of its influence and manipulated the royal houses of Europe
so that they conformed to the will of the Church. He was
not merely a successful politician; he sought to promote the
spiritual good of his people, and perhaps wrote the beautiful sequence: 'Veni, Sancte Spiritus'. The Albigensians
were the particular thorn in his side, as they had spread
from their strongholds in the Languedoc in France, through
the Pyrenees, all along the Mediterranean and into Italy.

As the Albigensians believed in a dual universe created
by one good and one evil spirit, all existence was a conflict
between these two principles. There were different inter-
pretations of the status of the devil; some held that he was a
co-equal son with Jesus, others that he was a fallen angel,
as were Adam and Eve, whose carnal appetites he had
excited. It was these carnal appetites that they held to be
original sin. They denied the dual Divinity and Humanity
of Jesus, who was considered only the highest of the Angels. Since he was not thought to have a material body,
they accused the Church of manufacturing the events of the
Crucifixion – and if there were no Crucifixion, there could
be no Resurrection, so the Church that taught these doctrines was considered to be the Scarlet Woman of the
Apocalypse. This made the heresy very popular with war
lords, who were delighted to find a cast-iron excuse for
robbing rich ecclesiastical foundations.

The Eucharist was denounced as an impostor, since
Jesus who was spirit, could not appear under the material
forms of bread and wine. Even the Cross was regarded as

evil. The elite amongst them were known as the Perfect, who refrained from sexual relations (including matrimony) and all forms of food that were the result of coupling. The weaker majority were called Believers, who could become Perfect by receiving a travesty of the sacrament of Extreme Unction at the point of death. All wars were considered evil, and capital punishment was an abomination.

Less numerous than the Albigensians, but equally opposed to the Church, were 'The Poor Men of Lyons' who originated as followers of a merchant of that city, Peter Waldo. He had a conversion experience in 1170, sold all he had and gave it to the poor. He translated the Gospels and several other books of the Bible into the vernacular, and became a familiar figure on the streets of Lyons, dressed like John the Baptist and denouncing the Clergy for being too lax. Gradually he attracted a number of followers, equally disenchanted with orthodox Catholicism, most of them poor and uneducated.

They were rabidly anti-clerical, and rejected most of the Sacraments, belief in purgatory, miracles, fasts and abstinences, and the convocation of the Saints. Since they bound themselves to tell the truth at all times, they claimed that all oaths, so vital in mediaeval society, were unnecessary. They were in fact Protestants and Puritans out of their time; sober and exemplary citizens. Pope Innocent, who excommunicated them, always hoped that they would be reconciled to the Church. It is interesting that when Francis began his mission, it was confused with that of the Waldensians – though of course Francis was particularly anxious to remain within the Church and accepted her doctrine.

Innocent III did his best to settle the question of the heresies by sending Papal Legates into the Languedoc. Inevitably they travelled in some pomp, and incurred the derision of those convinced admirers of the poverty and sincerity of the heretics. The head of the delegation, De Castelnau, excommunicated the Albigensian leader, Raymond of Toulouse, who retaliated by assassinating him.

71

Forced into a show of strength, Innocent III laid an interdict on his lands, absolved his vassals of their oaths of allegiance, and a crusade against Raymond was launched by the head of the Cistercian order. Simon de Montfort was prevailed upon to head the Crusade, and the vengeance wreaked by his armies was ferocious. The sacking of the town of Beziers was particularly savage; regardless of their affiliations, thousands of the townspeople were slaughtered and their homes burnt. More fortunate heretics were penalised by fines, exile or exclusion from public office; their rights of inheritance and their civic rights were withdrawn.

Meanwhile Dominic, dedicated to conversion by argument, reached the South of France in 1206. Eleven years later he was saying grimly: 'Where blessings can accomplish nothing, blows may avail.' This was the year when Marseilles had driven out its Catholic Bishop and desecrated the Eucharist – the ultimate sacrilege in the land where it was particularly venerated. The friars were considered to be the most suitable Orders to fight the heretics, as they had no local connections; but it soon ceased to be a battle about heresy. The war lords were paying off old scores, and plundering the rebel cities. In 1218, while his army was encamped at the gates of Toulouse, Simon de Montfort was killed by a stone from a giant catapult. After five years, Honorius II, the current Pope, decided to make one last attempt to rule with clemency, and sent in the friars once again. This time Francis had a new weapon to offer him; the ready tongue and quick wits of his 'Bishop' Anthony.

When he reached the Languedoc, Anthony found a territory roamed by wolves and wild boar, criss-crossed with rivers and lagoons in the magic atmosphere of the Mediterranean coast. This had been the land of the troubadours, who sang of love and war and chivalry, until they were swept away by the cruel reality of the Albigensian crusades, and it was their tradition of a wandering life which had so captivated Francis as a young man. The language of the region was a mixture of French, Provencal and Spanish

72

– the 'Langue d'Oc' – 'Oc' being the word for 'yes', as opposed to the more usual French 'oui'. As the trade routes were centred on the Mediterranean ports, there were people from all the regions of the known world, coming from North Africa, the Middle East, and the lands ruled by Genghis Khan on the Caspian Sea.

Anthony's first port of call appears to have been Montpellier, which belonged to the Kings of Aragon; hence the Spanish element in the vernacular, which would have been familiar to him. The proximity to the lagoons meant that frogs robbed the inhabitants of sleep, and Anthony won widespread gratitude by silencing them – though history does not relate how he managed it.

He was briefed to teach theology in the Franciscan monastery there, and then went on to enthral the citizens as he had done in Italy. The Muslims, who had recently vacated the town, had left behind flourishing schools of law and medicine. Among the students there were many whose youthful idealism posed a threat to the establishment. Anthony's own enthusiasm began to make inroads among them, and he won over an appreciable number.

Still young himself, he had a wisdom beyond his years, as a legend set in Montpellier shows. It has the fascination of a pious detective story, and the solution has all the symmetry and neatness of the genre. It might be called 'The Case of the Missing Psalter', since it concerns the fate of Anthony's own book. Any volume, patiently copied from existing manuscripts, and often embellished with exquisite decorations, would have been valuable, but this one was unique, because he had incorporated into it all the notes he used in his teaching.

One day he could not find it, and he must have been distraught. What aroused his suspicions was that a member of the noviciate had also disappeared. The Order was growing so rapidly, it drew its members from all walks of life, from the well-educated to those who could barely make their mark. Anthony knew it was possible that one of his colleagues could have coveted the book, but if it were found in his possession it would be an instant proof of guilt. It was much more likely that the missing novice had purloined it. Some were barely-reformed villains, who only took the habit to give an air of respectability to their vagabondage. In the eyes of the world, a Friar Minor was a notch above ordinary beggars. Instead of raising a hue and cry, and losing his temper as well as his treasure, Anthony did something only a saint would do; he resorted to prayer, and awaited events.

The action now passes to the flight of the villain, who was aiming for the River Lez. If he could get to the coast and take a ship, he would find a buyer for his all-too-traceable loot in a distant country. It seems that the river was in flood; the bridge at a suburb called Lattes was awash, barring his escape. Evidently this deterrent prodded his conscience, because one version of the story mentions the appearance of the devil in person – always a spur to the mediaeval mind. Whatever he faced on that stormy road made him turn tail and go back to the monastery, where he threw himself on the mercy of the book's owner, who always treated everyone with courtesy – even the heretics he argued with. The novice's desperate move was justified; not only was he forgiven, he was taken back into the noviciate, and became an exemplary friar.

As this story was repeated and elaborated over the years, it gradually became the custom to have recourse to Anthony in cases of loss. There is no doubt whatever that a moment of prayer and recollection is a more sensible solution to this kind of problem than frantic and ill-considered search, and Anthony's kindliness and humour towards his clients is reminiscent of his forbearance with the renegade novice. To this day, the bridge that was the scene of his repentance is still pointed out.

There is another example of his power that is said to have taken place at Montpellier. He was preaching in church, which he was often invited to do, although at the height of his popularity we are told that the churches could not accommodate all the crowds who wanted to hear him, and he was forced to preach in market-places, and in amphi-theatres and arenas left over from the Roman occupation of the region. When he began his sermon he immediately captured the attention of his congregation, but a little later they were alarmed to see him lean on the pulpit as if he were preparing for sleep, covering his head with his cowl. Since he showed no sign of distress, no-one thought to ask if he needed help. After a short time he threw back his cowl and resumed his sermon exactly where he had left off. Meanwhile the brothers at the Franciscan Monastery were singing the Mass. It was Anthony's turn to sing the Alleluia, and at the beginning of the service he was missing. But before a substitute had to be found, he appeared, added his part to the liturgy, and went out again when it was over.

It was not the only time when he was reported to be in two places at once; altogether three incidents of this kind are recorded. It has been recognised that some very holy people are capable of such a phenomenon. What is interest-ing about Anthony is that his appearance was not wraith-like, or mysterious in any way. Rather than let his brothers down, he simply repaired his fault with as little fuss as possible; quietly withdrawing himself in front of the crowd, and by the power of his thought projecting himself back to the monastery for just as long as his presence was needed. Many accounts of the abnormal happenings that have grown up around him have similarly matter-of-fact details re-corded, making them sound authentic. Even those much less credible have a core of truth; both types are offered us, for our own judgement.

Anthony was revered by his contemporaries for his quality as a preacher, his championship of the poor, the sanctity of his spiritual life, and the warmth with which he responded to requests for help. They did not need miracles to convince them that he was a remarkable human being. But after eight hundred years the miraculous element in his story persists, accruing new manifestations over that length of time. Without miracles, Anthony would still have his devotees; with them, he is irresistible.

Montpellier was a stronghold of the Orthodox Catholics, where in 1224 a council had been held in an attempt to win over Raymond VII, Count of Toulouse, to expel heresy from his domains and restore Church rights. The pressure was such that he gave this undertaking, and Anthony was under his protection when he went to Toulouse, an Albigensian stronghold. The province was still unsettled, and it took the utmost courage to visit the city, for Toulouse was at the heart of the heretical territory. Most of the town was built in the distinctive pink brick of the region, like Albi, with whom it shares a history of dark religious wars, each episode ending in the massacre of its citizens.

Like Montpellier, Toulouse housed a university; Honorius II had been instrumental in bringing professors from Paris to found the institution in 1217, but it had declined in prestige. Anthony taught theology in the Friary, as well as continuing his apostolate as a preacher. The present University dining-room is said to be the refectory of the old Friary. He would have preached in the beautiful Romanesque church of St Sernin, dominating a street running down to the bridge over the Garonne, its octagonal tower looming large above the meaner houses surrounding it. He may even have argued with the heretical Bishop Guillabert de Castres. Then at the Chapter of the Province of Narbonne, held in September 1225, he was elected Guardian at the Convent of Puy-en-Velay.

This meant another long, tiring journey into the mountains of the Massif Central, taxing his health which had never been robust, and was now further undermined by the days of fasting and nights of watching that he imposed upon himself. But – experienced traveller though he was – he must have been overwhelmed by the sight of the little town nestling in the dried-up bed of an enormous lake, surrounded by extinct volcanoes, each with its saucer-shaped depression at the top. The church of St Michel D'Aiguille, reached only by climbing over two hundred and fifty steps, is still perched high on its rock, clinging to it perilously, as if defying gravity. Another climb, up yet more steps, reaches the great Romanesque Cathedral in the heart of the town; a place of pilgrimage dedicated to Our Lady, which must have pleased him.

He delighted to do Our Lady honour, and it was reported of him that he was always distressed that in France the doctrine of the Assumption was considered doubtful. At that time it had not been defined by the Holy See, and it was not an obligation to observe it. Nevertheless, the Assumption was a great feast, although the Mass of the Vigil indicated that the Church in France remained silent on the subject. Once, during his stay, Anthony heard the bell for Prime, and decided that he did not want to listen to what he considered a slight to Our Lady, so – and we must remember that he was a model of adherence to the Rule – he absented himself from the Office. He was probably disciplined for this act of defiance, but it is reported that Our Lady consoled him with a vision of herself as a reward for his filial piety. Azavedo, the chronicler of the event, claims that Anthony personally annotated his description. This is pushing the evidence rather too far, since we are entirely in the dark about Anthony's handwriting; he almost certainly dictated the record we have of his sermons, copying then being considered work for less gifted friars.

It was at Le Puy that he was stopped by a pregnant woman who had evidently heard that he had the power of divination – and she asked if he would tell her the sex of the child she was expecting. She may have been well-to-do, and wanted a son to inherit land or a title, or to please her husband by providing him with an heir. Anthony, who seems always to have done his best to accede to direct requests, prayed briefly and then assured her that the baby would indeed be a boy. But he added that, far from succeeding to an earthly fortune, he would not only become a member of the Order of Friars Minor – he would win the crown of martyrdom. It was hardly the answer his mother expected, and she must have heard it with some misgiving. It is to be hoped that she became reconciled to his fate, because the story goes that in due course she had a son whom she named Philip, who became a friar and went to the town of Azot, in Saracen territory. Anthony had said that by his preaching he would lead many of the faithful to surrender their souls joyfully to martyrdom, and Philip requested his executioners to put him to death last, so he could encourage the others.

Another story told of Anthony's time in Le Puy, was that of the notary, who was rather worldly and of doubtful honesty, yet Anthony insisted on saluting him in the street with the utmost reverence. At first the recipient of this mark of regard was merely embarrassed, but it happened every time they met – which was frequently, for the town was a small one. He became more and more angry, suspecting that Anthony was mocking him. Indeed Anthony's sense of humour being very personal, it was not always possible to discern exactly what he was laughing at, but it is certain that he would not treat sincere or humble people in that way, although the worldly-wise might be fair game. Eventually, after yet another encounter, the notary decided that he would put a stop to Anthony's behaviour, and rounded on him, asking why he was being subjected to this unwelcome subservience? Anthony immediately confided to him his own early ambition to meet death at the hands of the Saracens, and said that he had been unsuccessful, but the notary would achieve what he had not. He added: 'And when this crown shall be given you, then remember me, I beg you, and pray for me.'

The notary dissolved into derisive laughter, refusing to believe that he was of the stuff from which Martyrs were made – but Anthony showed a greater insight into his character. Several years later the Bishop of Le Puy called for volunteers to go on a crusade. Whatever his motives, the notary promised his services, and was killed by the Saracens. All those who died in the Crusades were considered martyrs, so Anthony's prediction was fully justified. It was said of the notary that he preached Christianity to the Muslims with a convert's zeal, outdoing the Bishop in his condemnation of Islam. Anthony always took serious things seriously, and if envy ever entered into such a soul, it was of martyrdom that he was jealous.

In November 1225, Anthony attended a Synod at Bourges, between the rivers Cher and Loire. He was present as Custodian of the city, with charge of several convents under the Provincial, which shows the great confidence his superiors had in him. The position, which he combined with his preaching and teaching, would have demanded tact and responsibility. The Synod varies in importance, depending on the chronicler who recorded it; one says that six archbishops were present, a hundred bishops, and numerous priests and Abbots, as well as Raymond VII, Count of Toulouse, and that a crusade against the Albigensians was the matter in hand. A more modest gathering is indicated by another account, which tells that the Synod was held to reform abuses which had crept into the Church, and to settle the claims of overlords, resulting from the local religious wars.

Whatever the business of the gathering, Anthony was called upon to preach. The presiding bishop, Simon de Sully, a friend of Pope Honorius III, was not fond of the Friars Minor, sharing a current prejudice against what he considered their dangerous innovations. Without naming him, Anthony referred to: 'You, bearing the mitre' – which was less personal than it sounds, since many mitres were sported on this occasion. Anthony called upon him to acknowledge that there were misdeeds 'which lay upon his conscience'. This extraordinary frankness was not typical of his general attitude to authority, and he must have sensed that the cleric was genuinely troubled in mind, for we are told that the Bishop sought him out after the sermon was over, repenting in tears, confessing his faults and promising amendment. Later he became a friend of St Louis of France, who succeeded to the French throne in the following year when he was only eleven, and seemed doomed – since the fate of royal minors was often obscure, if not violent. However, with the help of his pious mother, Blanche of Castile, he lived to be a wise and resourceful monarch.

Simon de Sully not only gave him advice without fear or favour – as Anthony had advised him – but also became a good friend to the Friars Minor.

Bourges is one of two places in which the celebrated miracle of the Pious Mule is sited, the other being Rimini. The story begins with a man who argued with Anthony on the question of Transubstantiation. This doctrine was denied by the Albigensians, because they held all matter to be evil, so Jesus, who in their eyes was spirit alone, could not enter the material elements of bread and wine. Anthony declared categorically that 'On the altar there takes place the Transubstantiation of the bread and wine into the flesh and blood of Jesus Christ. The body which the Virgin begot, which hung on the Cross and was placed in the sepulchre, which rose again the third day and ascended to the right hand of the Father – this body, the Church today and every day presents and distributes to her faithful. When the priest speaks the words: "This is my body", the essence of the bread is turned into the Body of Christ.'

The unbeliever of Bourges – or as it might be, Rimini – refused to accept that anything had taken place, as he only credited the evidence of his own eyes. Anthony then offered to provide that evidence. He shared Francis's view that the lower animals had a prominent position in creation, unlike the heretics who held that they were not made by God. This was something more powerful than merely being fond of animals; both Francis and Anthony seemed to feel a bond with the innocence of those creatures that had not learned deviousness from their human masters; hence Francis's sermon to the birds, and Anthony's haranguing the fishes. This mule, however, was a more sophisticated beast. Anthony declared that at his request even the cynic's own animal would show its devotion to the Blessed Sacrament, by adoring it before witnesses.

The owner remained sceptical, but laid down conditions for the contest between his freethinking liberalism and the friar's orthodoxy. The mule was not to be given any food for three days preceding the experiment, and before he was

80

confronted with the Eucharist he should be offered some hay, in order to show his preference. Three days later, a great crowd assembled in a square near the church, all agog to know the outcome. The mule was led forth, ravenously hungry, and as is the way of mules, somewhat irritable. Anthony advanced from the church, carrying the Blessed Sacrament in a chalice. The mule's owner waved some fragrant hay beneath its nose; for a long moment, the crowd held its breath. Slowly, with reverence, the mule turned away and knelt on its forelegs in a gesture of devotion. The crowd gasped, and then greeted Anthony rapturously. After that, the sceptic abandoned his previous convictions, and became a devout believer. It was also a lesson to any incipient heretics who did not acknowledge that the animal kingdom was created by God.

Better authenticated, though equally mysterious, is the story of the Chapter at Arles, in Provence. With its partially demolished Roman arena and theatre, Arles was a centre of trade between Italy and the rest of the known world. As Custodian of Bourges, Anthony was present at the Chapter, and was preaching at a convent near the Cathedral of St Trophine, the legendary figure said to have been sent by St Peter to evangelise Provence during the Roman occupation. It was the Feast of the Exaltation of the Cross, and he chose as his text the inscription: 'Jesus of Nazareth, King of the Jews'.

He told how, in his Passion, Jesus was mocked by the soldiers with the purple robes, sceptre and crown of thorns. This reminded Anthony of the story from Judges, about the trees of the forest when they were offered Kingship. One after another, they refused it; the olive would have had to give up its oil – the fig tree would have had to give up its fruit – the vine would have had to give up its wine – and at last the bramble was approached. It said: 'If indeed you mean to make me King, come and rest under my shadow; but if you do not mean it, let fire come out from me, and burn the cedars of Lebanon.'

The way in which he led his listeners from the crown of

thorns to the story of the bramble is very typical of his style, especially as he went on to link the Old Testament story with the Christ of the New Testament, who was King of all the trees. He said that the devil could be described as a bramble; at first taken for a green herb, then stiffening and becoming thorny. 'The devil flatters the sinner, only to end by tyrannising him and making him feel the prick and prod of the thorn.' There, one feels, speaks a man who has gathered berries in a thicket.

As he preached, Monaldo, one of the brothers, looked up and saw a vision of Francis high above Anthony, stretching out his hands in blessing, showing the stigmata that he normally hid from everyone. It was known that Francis was in Assisi, and too ill to travel. His mystical appearance, encouraging Anthony in his mission, is well attested, and Francis admitted the experience before his death.

It was probably during this Chapter that Anthony was made Custodian of part of the Limousin Province, based on Limoges. He is credited with being the first Franciscan to take up this appointment, and Pierre Coral, the Abbot of St Martin's; wrote, soon after Anthony's death, that he had given him a lodging-place for his friars. In return, Anthony preached to them on the text: 'Who will give me the wings of a dove, that I may fly away and be at peace.' It is also known that he preached in the cemetery on All Souls Day, at the blessing of the graves. On that occasion his text was: 'Weeping endureth for a night, but joy cometh in the morning.' This made a great impression, and ensured a crowd of devoted followers wherever he went.

Limoges has two centres – the City, with its ramparts guarding the Cathedral, and the Town, with its commercial district of narrow streets lined with shops of all trades. Among them were the enamellers, whose delicate craft began about the time Anthony made it his headquarters. His stay was marked by several unusual happenings which were thought worthy of record. One was remarkably like the episode at Montpellier, when his two duties had clashed. On Holy Thursday he was preaching at the church of St

Pierre-de-Queyroix, at the highest point of the town. The huge space, wider than its length, under a low vaulted roof with round pillars, was packed with people. Suddenly they saw him pause, put his cowl over his face, and withdraw into himself. At this moment, in the monastery ten minutes away, where the friars were saying Matins, he appeared in his place and walked to the lectern where he was supposed to be singing one of the lessons. The scripture proclaimed, he resumed his place for a moment, and then vanished. While this was happening the vast congregation in St Pierre, who had been enthralled by his sermon, watched and waited until he threw back his cowl and picked up his discourse where he had left off. Friends of Anthony will recognise this as typical of the man, for the mark of his personality is on it – the double commitment, the fulfilment of both as unobtrusively as possible, and a touch of humour particularly his own.

The crowds that followed him grew greater than ever; one was estimated at thirty thousand, and he had to give up all thought of finding buildings large enough to accommodate them. At Limoges he led them to a Roman amphitheatre at the top of a hill called the Creux des Arenes. As he spoke, the sky darkened alarmingly, the air grew oppressive and the crowds began to panic. As lightning began to flash and ominous rumblings of thunder were heard, Anthony broke off to calm them, assuring them that the storm would not harm them; and in fact the ground where they were gathered remained dry. When they left, they discovered that the surrounding countryside had been saturated by torrential rain. Rigaud, the chronicler to whom we are indebted for many stories of Anthony's life, said that he had heard this from friars who were present at the time.

On another occasion, Anthony was preaching at a fairground in St Junien en Haut Vienne – a field where fairs are still held to this day. A makeshift pulpit had been erected; it was poorly made, and shook under Anthony's weight. People in the immediate vicinity were threatened by its collapse, and he assured them that although it would break, no-one would be hurt, not even himself. When this prediction came true, the crowd were shocked into silence, convinced that they had witnessed a miracle. Another of his al fresco sermons was heard by a woman who thought she would miss it, because she had to look after her sick husband. Opening her window, she heard him perfectly, even though he was two miles away.

There are two stories about women who were caught up in the prevailing excitement, so anxious to hear him, they left their children unattended. One returned to find her son dabbling his fingers in a boiling cooking-pot, without any appearance of harm. The other child was even younger; his mother left him in his cradle while she listened to the sermon, and when she returned her baby was dead. Running back to Anthony in tears, she beseeched him to help her. He had to repeat three times: 'Go, for God will show you his mercy', before her distress abated enough for her to take in his message. Hurrying back to the child, she found him alive, playing with some pebbles. Other holy people have revived the dead; only Anthony would have thought of the pebbles.

Another enthusiastic follower spent so much time helping the Franciscans that her husband grew jealous. When she made the mistake of trying to justify herself, he lost his temper completely and started dragging her about by her hair, pulling it out by the roots. She waited until she was alone, then sent for Anthony, saying that she was ill. Thinking she was in need of Extreme Unction, he was rather put out to find her apparently in good health, apart from the loss of some of her tresses, and did not show her much sympathy.

When he got back to the monastery, he had a change of heart, and asked the community to pray for her. Not only was her hair restored to its former glory; when she told her husband what had happened, he repented of his show of violence and became a good friend to the friars.

Around this time, Anthony's own health broke down; he was beginning to suffer from dropsy, a symptom of the disease that was eventually to prove fatal, and he was nursed in the Benedictine Abbey at Solignac, between Limoges and Brive. The abbey church, which he came to know well, has been preserved; a plain, uncluttered building flooded with light from high windows. The infirmarian was in the grip of great temptations; when Anthony became aware of this, he offered him his worn Franciscan tunic to wear. At the touch of the rough serge, the monk felt his torment subside, never to return.

When he was strong enough, Anthony travelled on to Brive, entrenched behind its ramparts. He is supposed to have made his home in a cave, now consecrated as a chapel, marked by a tablet. He also founded a monastery, but as it was in a remote spot, offerings were few, and the friars had a long way to go in search of food. Anthony nevertheless sent one of them to a lady who had already given them vegetables from her garden. She prevailed upon her maidservant to go and pick some more, but the weather broke and the girl had to gather them in pouring rain. But neither then, nor as she took them to the monastery, did she get in the least wet.

Anthony always showed great compassion for the brothers in times of temptation or aridity. One was a newly-accepted novice who was finding difficulty in adjusting to the religious life, and felt he must give it up. Anthony took him aside, breathed into his mouth, and said: 'Receive the Holy Spirit'. The man's doubts were put at rest, and he remained happily in the Order until his death.

It was Anthony's custom to meditate between Compline and Matins, which was said at midnight. One evening he was called away from his devotions, because the field of one of their benefactors, which was ripe for harvest, was being devastated by some vandals. Calmly and quietly, he said that there was no cause for alarm; it was a stratagem of the devil to interrupt their prayers, and the field was perfectly safe. In the morning, no damage was visible, and the corn rippled in the wind, quite unharmed. The brothers were convinced that they had witnessed a miracle.

It is not unknown for the insane to focus their fantasies on public figures. A poor soul, troubled in this way, followed Anthony about, muttering and shouting out during his sermons. From the pulpit, Anthony asked him courteously and gently to stop his interruptions. 'I cannot,' the man shouted, 'unless you give me the cord you wear as a girdle.' The cord, which was the badge of poverty, was very dear to a Friar Minor, but Anthony untied his and came down from the pulpit to give it to him. The man kissed it, and immediately became perfectly reasonable, with no recurrence of his former mania.

Between Limoges and Eymoutiers is the Castle of Chateauneuf-la-Foret, and the lord of the castle offered hospitality to Anthony when he was on his travels through the region. Observing his guest, he was greatly intrigued by his evident holiness, and was tempted to eavesdrop on his prayers. Standing outside the door of Anthony's room, he saw through a chink that it was suffused in a warm glow. When he peeped in, he was amazed to see Anthony cradling a very beautiful child in his arms, with tenderness and deference. He felt convinced that it was the Infant Jesus, and tackled Anthony about it the next day. Whether Anthony owned to the divine visitor or not, he extracted a promise of silence from his host, who only reported it after Anthony's death. The story is repeated in other locations, but it is so persistent that it seems that something like it must have occurred at some time, somewhere.

As the years passed, the religious wars that had brought ruin to so many were ended by the Treaty of Poitiers. This united Jane of Toulouse in marriage with Alphonsus of Poitiers, the brother of Louis IX, and brought peace to the South. The Albigensian heresy, already weakened by Anthony's efforts, faded into history.

But by then Anthony had long since left the Limousin. In 1226, he and the Order of Friars Minor were to receive bad news, which was to end his apostolate in France; news that was not unexpected – but none the less devastating for that.

The recall to Italy

All through the Christian world, wherever the Friars Minor had set up a Province, a copy of a letter was received by all the Superiors. In Brother Elias's impeccable Latin, it gave the sad news:

'Alas, the evil I so much dreaded has burst upon us; he who was our stay and consolation is no more; the pastor who bore us like lambs in his arms has departed to a far country; dear to God and to men, he has entered into the abode of light. We should rejoice for him, but we should weep for ourselves, for without him we are involved in darkness and in the shadow of death. Pray to him therefore that you may have a share in his glory; and beseech him to place at your head a valiant chief who may lead us forth to battle.'

He added: 'A short time before his death, our Brother and Father was seen to be like the crucified, having in his body the five wounds that are the marks of Christ' – with a description of the stigmata, quite obviously by one who had seen them.

Elias concluded with a call to a General Chapter to be held at Pentecost the following year, 1227, to elect a new Minister General. As Custodian of Limoges, Anthony was bound to attend.

The death of Francis had not been an easy one. His body in torment from the pressure of his dropsical limbs and his sight gone, he was brought forty miles from Rieti in Latinium, where he had received treatment for his illness, back to Assisi. The inhabitants of his native town were unwilling for his body to lie in alien soil; a great saint was a municipal blessing, bringing a steady stream of pilgrims with full purses.

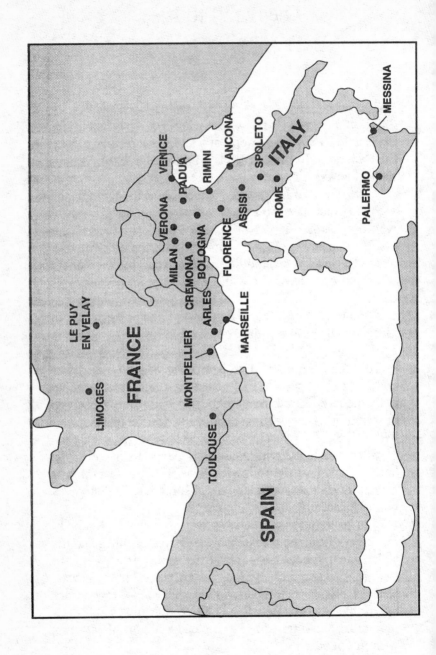

Francis was unable to walk or ride; he had to be carried in a litter by four of the brothers especially close to him, travelling slowly and avoiding towns and villages where the people might hasten his death through the enthusiasm of their greeting.

He worried incessantly about the care that he was receiving. In the words of Thomas of Celano: 'Even when his body was exhausted, he could not give it even a little relief without his conscience murmuring.' Austerity had become a habit, and he could not take advantage of the delicacies so anxiously pressed upon him. Then a young friar had an inspiration; he called on Francis to remember the good service his body had given him in the past, and told him to treat it well, now that it was exhausted and in pain.

This released him to accept everything that was offered with his accustomed courtesy – even a military escort, necessitated by an impending war between the Lombard towns, the Pope and the Emperor. As he travelled he became dehydrated, causing him further torment; his body shrunk to a skeleton and his skin unnaturally dark. One of the brothers – knowing that Francis, like Anthony, had longed for martyrdom – asked him which was worse; his present suffering or death at an executioner's hands. Francis's reply was a measure of his pain: 'Three days of this is harder to bear than any martyrdom could be.'

He was taken to the palace of Bishop Guy of Assisi. There his doctor, Buongiovanni of Arezzo, who had earned one of Francis's nicknames – 'Bembegnati' or 'Well-beloved' – replied to the question: how long would he have to endure his present agony? The doctor gave it as his opinion that he would die in a matter of weeks, at the end of September or the beginning of October. Francis greeted the verdict in characteristic fashion. To his masterpiece, 'The Canticle of Brother Sun', he added the lines:

'Praise be, my Lord, through our Sister Bodily Death
From whom no man living can escape.

Woe to those who die in mortal sin!
Blessed those whom she finds doing your most
   holy will
For the second death will do them no ill.

Praised and bless my Lord
And render thanks, and serve Him with great
   humility.'

The whole Canticle, his hymn of praise to his creator, was sung repeatedly, as it gave him comfort and pleased the guard set over him to prevent the access of unauthorised visitors. He, who had roamed the world so freely as the ambassador of his Lord, was now reduced to being the prisoner of his own fame.

The guard accompanied him back to his beloved Portiuncula. On the way he is reported to have asked that the litter should be set on the ground outside the leper house, so that he could bless the city. Some authorities have dismissed this detail because it only appears in later accounts, but it would be hard to rob the narrative of a parallel with Our Lord's blessing of Jerusalem. Francis's life was spent in the imitation of Christ, and he might have welcomed the opportunity to mirror him once again.

At the Portiuncula, he rested as well as he could in the atmosphere of coming and going, and was greatly refreshed by a visit from Jacoba of Settisole, who brought him some marzipan – his favourite sweetmeat – as well as his grave-clothes. On the evening of Saturday, 3rd October, he asked the brothers to sing 'The Song of Praise to the Lord, concerned with his approaching death', while he spoke with difficulty Psalm 141: 'I call upon Thee, O Lord, make haste to me.' He responded to a request for a last blessing to the Order; he forgave the friars all their faults and asked those about him to bless them all for him. He was determined to die in sackcloth, with ashes sprinkled over him, and his wish was respected. During the reading of the Passion of Jesus according to St John he breathed his last.

Anthony seems to have travelled to Italy by way of Marseilles, which had grown to accommodate fleets of ships, used by crusaders and pilgrims en route for the Holy Land. On his journey, he must have realised with a heavy heart that the blessing at Arles had been a farewell. By this time, many details of Francis's passing would probably have been known to him; in the mediaeval world the death of a saint was the stuff of legend, widely circulated. There would have been rumours about the contents of Francis's last testament, written when his death was inevitable; a document which Anthony would soon have cause to study with special attention.

One memorable incident took place on the way to Marseilles. Anthony and his socius found a lodging with a poor woman who, though hospitable, was an extremely nervous hostess. Eager to offer them wine, she drew some from a cask in her cellar, and accidentally left the tap on; then, oblivious of the leakage, she hurried upstairs to set the jug of wine and her only glass goblet on the table. When fumes from the wine rose from the cellar, her negligence was discovered; she became very agitated, and her nervousness was transmitted to Anthony's companion. In his anxiety, he tightened his grip on the glass, so that the stem snapped from the bowl.

Anthony alone was unruffled by the situation, and covered his face with his hands, bowing his head over the table. To their astonishment, the woman and the socius saw the stem and the bowl move and join together. Half frightened and half delighted, the brother grasped the newly restored glass in his hands and shook it – and it remained whole. The woman served them their simple meal, and went to clear up the cellar as best she could, only to find that where it had been awash with wine, it was now perfectly dry, and the cask was filled to the brim with a splendid vintage.

The sea voyage to Italy would have been hazardous and uncomfortable, under sail in a merchantman, or in a galley with five or six men at each oar, sweating amidships.

Although his fame as a preacher was widespread, as a mendicant friar, Anthony travelled steerage, with the poorest of the poor.

Whether he sailed straight to the Tuscan coast – Livorno or Pisa, settled as seaports in the days of the Roman Empire – or headed for Ancona on the Adriatic, is not recorded. If he took the latter course, he might have broken his journey in Sicily, where he is supposed to have founded four convents, and this would appear to have been his only opportunity. The capital, Palermo, has a church named for him, and he is popular all over the island.

The Guardian at Messina, hearing that a famous preacher was in their midst, asked him to deputise for less gifted brothers. The friars had a long way to go to fetch water, so Anthony dug them a well; perhaps he had the power of water-divining, along with his other gifts. In any event, the Guardian was less pleased with this additional comfort than might have been expected. He was a fanatical adherent to the Rule of absolute poverty, and considered that Anthony had erred against it, depriving the brothers of merit. He disciplined Anthony severely, and remains the sole example of someone who failed to be impressed by him.

Two other incidents are credited to him, during his stay in Sicily. On one occasion the brothers were given a splendid capon on a Friday, when there was no other food available. Anthony ensured that they would be able to eat, by turning the capon into a large fish, sufficient for their needs. The other story concerns one of those tricks played on the brothers by local pranksters, who could not be commended for the subtlety of their wit. When they gave the brothers a dead owl as alms, Anthony turned the tables on them by changing it into an appetising joint of meat. Later writers dismiss these stories as smacking too much of conjuring tricks, but they still persist among the faithful, who perhaps remember the divine gift of water changed into wine at Cana.

When Anthony reached Assisi, in time for the Whitsun

Chapter of 1227, he found the sons of Francis drawn up into two camps; the Conventuals, and the Friars of the Strict Observance. Deprived of the restraining presence of their founder, no holds were barred in the struggle between them. Thomas of Celano tells how, when Francis was alive, he had been asked to name his successor, and had replied with deep sighs of regret that he did not see anyone capable of being the leader of an army with so many different recruits, or the shepherd of so large a flock, though he had very definite ideas about the kind of man such a leader should be.

Reading his specification, it is not difficult to see why no-one matched up to it. He asked for a man of discretion and good reputation, who would divide his time carefully between prayer, and the needs of the brothers; he also said that the brother selected should be a priest who could say Mass for the whole Order as his first act every morning, and make a long thanksgiving; that he should always be available to any of the brothers who needed him, whether simple or gifted; that he must wear his learning lightly, and not give himself over to study at the expense of his service to others. As the last resort of the afflicted, he should prevent them from giving way to despair. It would be better if he disliked taking up the office, which seems to rule out the ambitious; he must be kind, but keep the balance between laxity and discipline, so that he would be loved by all, yet keep authority over those who had evil tendencies.

It was for such a paragon that the brothers were searching, in their election for a Minister General. Elias, who had held the office since 1221, was looking to keeping it. Born in Assisi, like Francis, he came from a poor family of mattress-makers and had been apprenticed to the craft, but set up as a schoolmaster for those who knew even less than he did, moving on to Bologna, where he seems to have become a writer and copier, acquiring some learning on the way. He entered the Order when it was new and flexible and offered a self-educated man the means of obtaining influence more readily than one of the established foundations. He showed an early genius for organisation at a time when it was desperately needed, and was entrusted with important duties by Francis, all of which he executed with great success. On his deathbed, Francis blessed him especially, not only because of his position as Minister General, but because of his personal love and loyalty.

Those who opposed Elias seem to have been offended by a comparatively minor thing. He had set up a marble chest to gather the offerings of the faithful in order to build a basilica worthy of Francis. This was premature, and typical of the man – he knew it would be necessary, and started to organise it without reference to anyone else, the prime fault of executive directors. He would have made a valuable Canon Regular or Dominican, but he moved too far and too fast for the democratic Franciscans.

In his place, they elected a gentle, persuasive ex-Judge, John Parenti – exactly the sort of man to appeal to Anthony, who was to have his own disagreements with Elias, believing that the changes he wished to make should not be too radical, and instituted at a pace acceptable to the whole body of the Order.

John Parenti presided over the Chapter and saw that it tightened discipline, encouraged devotion to the Eucharist, decided not to accept indiscriminately every novice who offered himself, and forbade Friars Minor to take any title other than 'Brother'. No-one could object to any of these provisions, and they augured well for the new Minister General's period of leadership. Like the rest of the Order, Anthony must have sighed with relief. Elias was to be kept busy designing and organising his own project, a worthy resting-place for their Founder. Certainly his love for Francis was one of the best things about him. Anthony too received a new vocation; he was made Provincial of the huge territory known as Emilia Romagna.

Francis seems to have envisaged his ideal Minister-General to be, as the name suggests, one who acted as father to the Order and directed its affairs in a general way. The Ministers Provincial had to have all these virtues, and also be accessible to the Brothers, to rule with such kindness and affability that those who had failed would feel able to approach them and count on their goodwill. They should keep their commands to a minimum, and if they were wrong, acknowledge it cheerfully without any ill-will. Above all, they had to set a good example. Francis wanted them to act in such a way that the Brothers would love them; and as the Provincials had to bear many responsibilities for them, he promised that God would reserve great rewards for their fidelity to his precepts.

Immediately he was appointed, Anthony set about visiting his Province, which stretched from the northern border of Tuscany to the Tyrol, and from the Ligurian Sea to the Adriatic. The region was torn by heresy, and the long-standing war between Frederick II and the Papacy. In 1225 Frederick had married Isabella, heiress to the kingdom of Jerusalem; three years later he was ready to claim his title, and went to the Holy Land, though the reigning Pope, Gregory IX, a great friend to the Franciscan Order, had excommunicated him, and the Papal armies lay waiting to annexe his territories. He negotiated a settlement with the heir of Saladin, Francis's particular Sultan of Egypt, and obtained in addition to the coastal strip in Christian hands, Nazareth, Bethlehem and Jerusalem, and access to the port of Acre. He also seized the crown of the King of Jerusalem that was kept in the Church of the Holy Sepulchre, and placed it on his own head, as he could not find a single churchman to do it.

The quarrel between the Papacy and the Emperor caused civil war in almost every town and city, and whichever faction was in power harried the other, though the skirmishes were intermittent and would be halted for really important things like gathering the harvest or the festival of a saint. Heresy was a different matter, and these bitter struggles caused strong animosity, which festered away for years. There were also feuds between great families whose interests conflicted – as happened in Florence.

Florence was the native city of John Parenti, and in 1228

he particularly asked Anthony to preach a series of Advent sermons in the cause of peace, and succeeded in gaining a temporary respite in the hostilities. He was also invited to preach at the funeral of an exalted nobleman, and gave his relatives rather more than they had bargained for, choosing as his text: 'Where thy treasure is, there will your heart be also', and – a true son of Francis – painted a vivid picture of the nobleman's heart, still warm among the money in his coffers. Someone of a rather literal turn of mind actually went to look in the vault of the treasure-house, and managed to convince himself that he had seen the tell-tale heart – a story which ran through the city like wildfire.

In Ferrara, Anthony appeared in a very sympathetic light. During a domestic fracas, a jealous husband accused his wife of giving birth to a baby that was not his. Anthony intervened, calling on the tiny infant to witness to his mother's innocence. The baby received the power of speech prematurely, and pointed at the raging husband, saying quite clearly: 'You are my father' – whereupon the man was shocked out of any doubt about his child's parentage.

Anthony also made visits to Cividale, Treviso, Conegliano and Venice, where a memory lingers in a village named for him in a southern island of the Lido, facing the Adriatic. He was as popular there as he had been in Sicily, in spite of his sermons against the prevailing vices, corruption and licentiousness. He also warned his listeners about their tendency to recourse to moneylenders, in order to feed their appetite for expensive luxuries.

In the university city of Bologna, he wrote out some of his sermons on the Psalms and gave them to the Brethren, whose Lector he had been. Unfortunately they were misplaced in the Library and did not surface again until they were rediscovered by a Father Azzoguidi in the Eighteenth Century.

Milan had an expanding ghetto of Waldenses, whom Anthony strove to bring back into the fold of the Catholic Church. He was much harder on corrupt clergy, especially those who only said Mass when they were paid for it,

Bishops who bought and sold offices and abandoned their flocks to indulge in hunting, or leading private armies into skirmishes. He spoke out firmly against those who 'have hands to gather money, but not to touch the wounds of Christ. Thus the wolf, who is the devil, scatters the flock, and the thief, who is the heretic, makes off with it.'

He was a great man for practicalities, and once again discovered a hidden spring at Varese, digging a well that was immediately credited with restorative powers. This caused a great deal of jealousy in the neighbouring town of Brescia, so he blessed their principal reservoir, and when miraculous cures began to be reported there, honours were even between the towns.

In Gemona he set about building a convent, and to help the work along asked a man with a cart who was passing by to help in carrying some stones. The man was reluctant to comply, and pointed to his son lying asleep in the back of the cart, passing him off as a corpse he was taking for burial. Anthony accepted this, and the man went on to his destination, only to find when he attempted to rouse his son that he was indeed dead. Hurrying back to Anthony, he begged his pardon for the deception and begged his help, which was readily given, and the son revived.

On all these journeys he had the company of a very loyal and loving socius, Luke Pelludi, a convert of Francis himself, who cared for Anthony until his death. They travelled the rough terrain of the Province together, climbing mountains or traversing the damp plains. Sometimes, unable to find lodging at a monastery, they shared a barn with farm animals, or even bedded down in the open air with stones for their pillows. They ate what was given them by the faithful, who were nearly as poor as they were themselves. The man who could hold thousands enthralled by his sermons was often reduced to begging in order to keep hunger at bay. Sharing these experiences drew them close, and helped Anthony in the inevitable loneliness of his office. As St Bonaventure said later, whatever a Superior did, he could hardly ever satisfy everyone; someone could always be found to complain that he might have acted otherwise – and better – if he had wished. Anthony would frequently be in doubt whether he ought to yield to the Brothers' arguments and acquiesce in everything they wanted, or hold rigidly to what he believed to be expedient. Again, they would seize on things he did and interpret them in the wrong way, then seek him out to complain, or accuse and disparage him. What he thought to be of service to God, they held to be a stumbling-block, and he found the whole situation almost irredeemable, as everything he arranged or tried to do seemed to displease somebody.

It was very much against Anthony's temperament to be misunderstood in this way. He could thunder against heretics in his sermons, but in his personal relationships he hated to disappoint anyone, and he is often described as being anxious to put things right when they miscarried. Left to himself he was naturally charming and courteous, but his office demanded a toughness and ability to command others that did not come easily to him. On top of this, he had to fulfil his vocation to preach, as well as carry out his administrative work, which meant that he was always under a heavy strain.

He had great need of someone as devoted to him as Luke Palludi. Many years later their bones were laid to rest in Anthony's favourite city of Padua; when his time came, the modest socius was given a burial-place in his friend's Basilica, close to his shrine.

Anthony came to Padua in the year 1228, taking up residence for this first brief stay on the banks of the river Bacchiglione, and giving a course of Lenten sermons. Though he was now a long way from Assisi, it is very likely that he went back there to witness the canonisation of his beloved Francis on 16th July. The ceremony was to be performed by Pope Gregory IX, who – as Bishop of Ostia – had watched over the Order's progress from its beginnings. It was not only a mark of favour to an old friend; he had been obliged to leave Rome after an attack by the Emperor's forces.

The Curia had backed Elias in his desire to build a huge Basilica on a piece of land donated by Simone Pizerelli, a burgher of Assisi. It was not a prestigious location, being called 'Colle d'Inferno' – Hell hill – outside the west gate, but as in all hill cities, building land was hard to come by, and most of the more salubrious sites were already taken. The people of Assisi subscribed to a fund to raise a suitable monument for the relics of their beloved fellow-citizen, soon to be acknowledged by the Church as a saint, although in their eyes he was canonised already.

Pope Gregory used his visit to Umbria as a general show of strength. The actual consistory that was to examine Francis's life and work was held in Perugia; the miracles were read, although the Pope insisted it was not necessary, that his holiness was sufficient for Francis to be raised to the honours of the altar. Then he donned the papal crown and in vestments of cloth of gold, under a rich canopy, rode out to Assisi. He was surrounded by his court, many Cardinals and Bishops, all wearing white robes decked out with jewelled collars. Rome in all its glory came to the city of the man who had served Lady Poverty before everyone; the faithful son of the Church whose humility was legendary. It was a day to make Elias proud. At last the Order was being given its due as the greatest popular movement in the Church.

Anthony would have been standing with the other brothers at the church of St George, where Francis's emaciated body had been buried only two years ago. Their rough tunics tied with cords were in marked contrast to the prelates and the people of Assisi, all dressed in their best clothes, who had stripped branches from the trees, recalling the progress of Jesus into Jerusalem on Palm Sunday, twelve hundred years earlier. The sun itself – Francis's 'Lord Brother Sun' – shone so brightly, the jewels on display dazzled the onlookers.

A solemn pontifical High Mass was sung by specially trained choirs. When it came to the time for the homily, Gregory himself mounted the pulpit, taking as his text a verse from the Book of Ecclesiasticus: 'He shone in his days as the morning star in the midst of a cloud, and as the moon when it is full. And as the sun when it shineth, so shone he in the temple of God.' When he said these words the Pontiff broke down in tears. Haltingly he continued, his discourse punctuated by emotion which transmitted itself to his hearers. The people of Assisi grew restive as their expectations threatened to overwhelm them. They had been waiting in stifling heat for hour after hour, and their nerves were stretched to snapping-point.

But the great moment had not yet come. First the list of miracles had to be read and commented on by a Cardinal Deacon, Capocci of Viterbo, who had presided over the first Chapter that Anthony had ever attended, in 1221, when he was overlooked and friendless. This recital again provoked a display of emotion from those present; Assisi was within a hairsbreadth of becoming the greatest place of pilgrimage in Italy after Rome, ensuring its prosperity for many ages to come.

Then Gregory rose, and read from the Bull of Canonisation, held by an underling:

'To the praise and glory of Almighty God, the Father, and of the Son, and of the Holy Spirit, and of the glorious Virgin Mary, and to the honour of the glorious Roman Church; the most glorious father Francis, whom God has glorified in heaven, we venerate on earth, and by the counsel of our Brothers here present and other prelates, we decree that he shall be numbered in the catalogue of the saints, and that his feast shall be observed on the day of his death.'

The Te Deum heralded the new saint into the glorious company of the apostles; the crowd cheered and wept and cheered again. In the hubbub, the Pope left his throne and went down to kiss the grave of the Poor Man of Assisi. This homage must have moved Anthony and his companions more than anything that happened that day. Francis had met all men as brothers, and now the most powerful man on earth honoured his last resting-place. But that was to be only a temporary one. Elias had prepared the foundations of the new Basilica – the splendid, almost imperial, tomb he had envisaged. One Brother spoke out against its magnificence. Did Anthony echo his sentiment? In any event, Elias had his way.

The next day the Pope laid the foundation stone, Elias was free to build as he wished – and Anthony went back to his uncongenial task, to serve his Province faithfully, upheld by thoughts of his beloved father Francis, who was also misunderstood.

The road to Rome

Now the most important industrial centre of the Veneto, with its ugly suburban sprawl, it is difficult to imagine the Thirteenth Century city of Padua. It was originally settled during the time of the Roman Empire, when it had been a favourite resort of the Emperors, who lost it to the Lombards in the Seventh Century, and it obtained the status of a free city in the Twelfth. From this independence the people grew rich, and built extensively – too extensively. They were famous for the extravagance of their life-style and beggared themselves by resorting to moneylenders; interest at thirty per cent was common. The University, founded in 1221, had students with loans at twenty per cent, which was considered reasonable.

Although the city declared for the Pope, it was far from pious, and carried on a sporadic war with nearby Verona, which was not surprisingly a Ghibelline stronghold, its ruler being Ezzelino da Romano, the son-in-law of the Emperor Frederick II. He had succeeded in capturing some influential Paduans and held them in miserable conditions in his dungeons. Contemporary descriptions of Ezzelino dwell on his extreme cruelty, which he vented not only on his political enemies; among his prisoners was his own brother-in-law, the Count of San Bonifacio, who was well-known in Padua, and very popular. Anthony was sympathetic to his plight, and awaited an opportunity to intervene on behalf of him and his fellow-sufferers.

Although Padua was his base, and its people were dear to him, he did not cease to visit the other towns of his Province, giving a series of Advent sermons in Florence in 1228, and returning in the Lent of the following year with another course. It was not yet the splendid city that it was to become in the Renaissance, but already had an artistic life centred on its great churches and palaces. Anthony spoke out against corruption in high places, and drew enormous crowds.

But Padua is the scene of the most charming stories about him. Although he excelled in the pulpit, he was also in great demand as a confessor. A man who had been moved by his preaching to make what promised to be a long overdue confession found when his turn came that he was so nervous, he could not get a word out. Taking pity on him, Anthony encouraged him to write his sins down and read them. The young man took his advice, only to find that the writing had been expunged, because Anthony had forgiven his sins in advance of their disclosure.

One bright May day he preached in the open air from a bench suspended in an oak tree. His hearers gathered round him in enormous numbers, and a nearby field of wheat was trampled underfoot. Quite justifiably, the owner complained to Anthony about its loss. It is an example of Anthony's consideration for others that he immediately petitioned heaven for redress, and the next day the crop emerged, erect and unscathed.

There is a folk tale about an incredulous bystander who asked as the price of his belief that Anthony should prevent a glass being broken as he hurled it to the ground. Anthony's response was not only to preserve the glass, but to shatter the heavy flagstone it landed upon. Still unconvinced, the unbeliever demanded a further test. He held up the glass and a very withered piece of vine, and asked Anthony to make grapes grow on it, which would turn into wine and fill the glass. That, he insisted, would be something like a miracle. No-one knowing Anthony was in the least surprised when the piece of vine completed its cycle by producing grapes which ripened before their eyes, and were pressed into wine, filling the glass. The sceptic finally accepted this evidence, and remained to follow Anthony.

Some of his many converts asked him for a Rule that they could keep in the world, and when he complied they built a small church for themselves, dedicated to the Madonna della Colomba; they were known in the city as 'Colombini'. On the feast of St John, 27th December, Anthony delighted them by giving them a grey habit, fastened with a cord similar to that worn by the Friars Minor. He returned as often as his duties allowed to hear their confessions and urge them to penance and a virtuous life. They seem to have been similar to the members of the Third Order of St Francis, who had recently been made exempt from military duty by Pope Gregory IX, which made the Order more popular with converts than ever, and they set up a common fund to buy themselves out of military service, as they were entitled to do by the Papal authority.

When Anthony first settled in Padua there was only one small convent at Arcella, a mile outside the town; the home of the Friars who attended to the spiritual needs of a convent of Poor Clares. After a time Anthony, as Provincial, opened a larger foundation called St Mary's in the town itself, but if tradition is to be believed, he kept his connection with Arcella by becoming the confessor of Blessed Helena Enselmini, a patrician lady who was a member of the community. They were certainly resident in Padua at the same time, and both their names were added to the Confiteor when the nuns recited it, so in that way they were remembered together.

After the Lenten sermons in Florence of 1229, Anthony visited Milan which was torn by war between the followers of the Papacy, and those of the Emperor. The Imperial faction had allied itself with the Waldenses, but the civil authorities acted against the heretics. Eventually Frederick II formed a temporary alliance with Pope Gregory, in an effort to have the excommunication against him lifted. Strong measures could then be taken; even harbouring someone who had been excommunicated could result in a heavy fine. Anthony fought the heresy with all his intellectual and spiritual weapons, disputing with the deviants from orthodoxy, and through his clear explanation of the

Catholic faith caused many to return to the Church. He welcomed them with warmth and generosity, never penalising them for their infidelity.

The remainder of his tour took him once again to Vercelli, where his former mentor Dom Thomas had been Abbot of St Andrew's monastery for two years. He also made a return visit to Varese and Cremona, where he opened a new church for a monastery founded by St Francis, and dedicated it to the saint. He preached in all the principal cities of the region, and was often compelled by the numbers that wanted to hear him, to preach in the open air, but in one church a horseman rode up to the door at full gallop, sought out a matron in the congregation and gave her a letter, which created a great commotion. The woman read the letter, which told her that her son had been captured by his enemies and put to torture. Her emotion was audible, but she could not move in the packed church. Anthony had not been at all distracted by the incident – indeed it was believed that he was unaware of it – but when the sermon was over he sought her out, told her that her son was well and on his way back to her. He explained that the messenger was an agent of the devil, and said she was to pay no attention to him.

His final visitations included one to Verona, still an unhappy city, where he proclaimed the gospel to all without fear or favour – Julian, an early chronicler, records that he was 'Like a flaming torch in the eyes of the world.' Such outspokenness was dangerous, but that did not deter him, proving that he had lost none of his missionary zeal. He spent the Easter of 1230 in Mantua, where on Ascension Day the annual miracle of the liquefaction of the Precious Blood attracted hundreds of thousands of pilgrims, and then returned to Padua.

As he was walking through the town, he met a man called Peter, who was carrying his daughter Paduana in his arms. She was so handicapped that by the age of four she could only crawl on her hands and knees. She was also epileptic, and most probably a Down's Syndrome sufferer.

Her father begged the Friar to bless her, and Anthony, much moved by his not venturing to ask for an outright cure, readily signed her with the cross. When Peter reached home he set the child on her feet, placed a chair before her, and was rewarded by seeing her push it in front of her. As her legs grew stronger from this exercise, he gave her a stick instead of a chair, and in the end she was able to walk without any support at all. So far we can see the natural consequence of the application of physiotherapy to the case, but we are also told in the Primitive Legend that from the moment Anthony blessed her, she ceased to have any epileptic seizures. Benignitas tries to dramatise the incident by making the cure instantaneous, which loses both its charm and its credibility.

In addition to travelling and preaching, Anthony wrote down, at the request of the Lord Cardinal of Ostia, his sermons for the Sundays of the year, including one in praise of Mary, of which he writes: 'If you should find anything poorly presented or expressed in a dry and inadequate way, impute it to my inability, my blindness, my stupidity.' This, from the man who was continually praised for his eloquence. His humility was unassailable.

It began to be noticed that under the influence of his teaching, armed forays into the surrounding countryside ceased, and a new era of peace and plenty came to the city. Some earlier biographers also claimed that the weather was more clement, which was fortunate, since he so often delivered his sermons in market places and open spaces, or the fields outside the city walls. People got up before daybreak to obtain a good place, including the rich, who had a reputation for feasting all night and rising late. Even the shopkeepers closed their premises and joined their customers.

In less favourable weather, owing to the pressure of the crowds, one lady slipped and fell into a sea of mud. We know the kind of woman she was, because although she was afraid of being suffocated, she was still more anxious about the fate of the precious dress she had put on for the first time, in honour of the occasion. In tears, she appealed to Anthony, telling him that she feared the wrath of her husband who had paid so much for the dress. At the time, Anthony does not seem to have committed himself, but when she returned to face her husband, the garment was seen to be as good as new. Her neighbours who had witnessed the event credited Anthony with another of his obliging miracles, praising God for it and then hurrying off to hear his sermon.

Anthony himself had to run the gauntlet of people with scissors, who tried to cut off pieces of his habit, to be used as relics in all kinds of calamities, and he had to recruit a bodyguard of sturdy young men to preserve him from the over-enthusiasm of his clients.

In 1230 he was due to go to the Pentecost Chapter at Assisi. Brother Elias had surpassed himself in organising the building of St Francis's Basilica. He had planned an ambitious scheme of a double church on two storeys, and had made sufficient progress on the lower church for the relics of the saint to be placed within it; but Gregory IX, who was intending to be present at the ceremony, had to change his plans. Frederick II had returned to Italy in triumph from the Holy Land with a menagerie of exotic animals, including the first giraffes ever to be seen in Europe. An attempt was made to arrange a reconciliation between the Pope and his unruly son in God, and this had a prior claim, but Gregory sent handsome gifts by no less than three legates, and gave great privileges to the church. He granted the service of the church to remain in the hands of the Friars Minor in perpetuity; he himself had nominal ownership of the land, so that the rule of poverty should be preserved. He also granted indulgences to all those who visited the Basilica for the translation of the remains of St Francis, or any who made the journey before the nativity of Our Lady on 8th September. These indulgences were on a sliding scale, according to the distance travelled.

The ceremony was to take place on 25th May, the day after Pentecost, and it was to be the highlight of Brother Elias's career. He had almost literally moved mountains to achieve his goal. Subesio, which overlooked Assisi, was unstable, and Elias had ordered the construction of massive foundations to support the huge Basilica. But the citizens of Assisi fully intended to make their own bid to venerate the Poverello they regarded as their saint. On the Vigil of the Feast, a huge throng of the people – not only the poor who loved him, but the Governor, together with representatives of the Guilds and a full complement of the aristocracy – gathered in and around St George's church. In striking contrast to the brilliance of the assembled company, the simple wooden coffin was mounted on a decorated ox-cart, and the cortege set off for the new church.

What should have been a celebration of love for the saint was marred by scuffling amongst the crowd. Whether some marauders from a neighbouring city had joined them in an attempt to carry off the relics, or whether this was merely a rumour, the solemnity of the occasion was lost. The body was moved with unseemly haste to the Basilica, and the doors locked to prevent access by the mourners, who had by this time degenerated into a mob. They set up a clamour outside, during which the offices were gabbled and the coffin buried. Only the immediate bystanders knew exactly where it lay. Such secrecy was necessary in order to prevent grave-robbers from rival cities like Perugia and Spoleto, who would have been only too anxious to lay hands on these valuable remains. Even those near enough to witness the interment were too confused to remember the exact site afterwards, and for centuries the knowledge was lost, until in 1819 a committee of historians and archaeologists was set up by the Pope, empowered to make excavations and thus establish the authenticity of the coffin which is venerated to this day.

But not everyone was aware of the change of plan, and all through Pentecost Sunday the crowds continued to pour into Assisi. To avoid an eruption of lawlessness, the ceremonies had to take place as planned, and the solemn High Mass which took place in the presence of the Papal Legates, presiding over a brilliant assembly, was conducted by

John Parenti, the Minister-General of the Order of Friars Minor. This was not a plan that pleased everyone, and grumbling voices blamed Brother Elias for the decision to translate the body three days early. He protested that he had only done so to prevent their treasure falling into unconsecrated hands.

Whatever the rights and wrongs of the case, the Holy See threatened the townspeople with excommunication unless they amended their riotous behaviour, and various penalties were incurred by the Order, including a total ban on members entering the Basilica. When the people of Assisi apologised, the ban was lifted, but the fire was only damped down, not put out. Brother Elias had always been misunderstood, and during the Chapter that followed he did not help the situation by bringing up the question of Francis's Last Will and Testament.

This document appears to have been dictated by Francis on his deathbed. In it, he is anxious that it should not be observed as another Rule, but he sees the need for a statement about his first vision of the Order, as a band of brothers going out into the world with the commands of Jesus to his disciples engraved on their hearts. It must be remembered that his last illness caused him pain akin to martyrdom, which must often have interrupted the dictation, and that many of the brothers, including Elias who was at that time the Minister-General, had bypassed his wishes on the question of poverty and what it should mean within the Order.

Francis began with a brief reference to his own conversion, from a rich worldly youth with an abhorrence of leprosy to the ragged friar who entered the pesthouses to nurse the sufferers. He reiterated his respect for the priesthood, counting himself below them, because of their consecration to the Divine Office, and saying that for him they stood in the place of Christ. There was only one thing he saw worthy of a richly ornamented resting-place, and that was the Eucharist. Everything else the brothers used must be as poor and simple as possible. The pages of the scriptures, especially those bearing the Holy Name, must be respected; he had been seen to pick up such pieces of paper from the ground and put them carefully in a safe place, so they should not be desecrated.

Then he went back to the dawn of the Order, and told how they tried to live the Gospel life in piety and simplicity. Working with their hands was obligatory; those who did not know how to had to learn as he had, building the walls of derelict churches and undertaking menial tasks. When they could not find work, they begged for alms, and wherever they went they carried with them the greeting God had taught him: 'God give you peace.'

He repudiated everything that could lead to the ownership of property, but conceded that they could occupy premises temporarily, as 'strangers and pilgrims'. He forbade them to seek Papal protection and privileges, or ask for soldiers to guard them if they fell foul of the authorities while on foreign missions. He wished all the brothers to accept the discipline of the Order; malcontents were to be judged by the hierarchy, from the lowliest Custodian up to the Protector, the Lord Bishop of Ostia. He insisted that this document was merely a reminder of the previous Rule, that nothing should be added to nor abstracted from it, and that it should be read whenever the Rule was read. He ended with his last blessing to the brothers.

Elias's supporters were anxious to circumvent Francis's intentions and press for an amendment of the Rule. They continued to argue even when Elias himself was absent in his cell; then, thinking that only his election as Minister-General would ensure their success, they dragged him back to the Chapter by force in an attempt to depose John Parenti. In the melee which followed, when the unfortunate Brother John, either willingly or unwillingly was deprived of his tunic, it was generally realised that matters had gone too far. Thomas of Eccleston tells how five of the novices, who had been knights when they were in the world, pleaded in tears before the company that this fracas should cease, before the future of the Order was jeopardised.

There is a story, almost certainly apocryphal, about a heated exchange between Anthony and Elias, in which Anthony accused Elias of living in luxury, keeping a fine horse, and eating in private so that no-one could see whether his food had the proper Franciscan simplicity. There was a short but bitter exchange, during which Elias claimed that St Francis himself had mitigated the Rule in his case, by virtue of his office, and Anthony said that even if St Francis had meant him to relax the Rule, he had certainly not given him permission to live like a lord. This caused Elias to 'swell up with choler and bile', as the old account has it, and shout: 'You liar!'

Whether or not this altercation took place, both men gave up their offices; Elias retired to a hermitage where he became noted for the length of his hair and beard, as well as his sanctity. The unknown author of 'The Little Flowers of St Francis' paints a grimmer picture of his having left the Order to join Frederick II and suffer excommunication as a result, only to be recalled by invoking the prayers of St Francis. Perhaps this reflects the low ebb to which Elias's reputation had fallen, rather than strict historical fact.

Anthony petitioned Brother John Parenti, who was confirmed as Minister-General when the Chapter returned to the business in hand, to release him from his duties as Provincial of Romagna, so that he could devote his time to preaching and writing. Though he was in many ways an exemplary Provincial, punctilious in visiting the foundations under his care, as an administrator he seems to have been the proverbial square peg in a round hole, which is made apparent by his short stay in the post.

He was chosen, however, as one of a delegation to Rome, to ask the Pope for a ruling on the use in the Order of St Francis's Last Will and Testament, and he may well have earned his place in the party through the tactfulness and moderation of his views. Second to none in his reverence for St Francis, he also saw the need for amendment of the original Rule, to which the testament was a return. He had received the endorsement of his talent as a preacher by

St Francis's apparition at Arles, and sought no other position in the Order than the opportunity to exercise it. Another reason for his removal might well have been his health, which was giving anxiety, and he was indeed within a year of his death.

He had a powerful friend in Rome, no less than the Bishop of Velletri and Ostia, the nephew of Pope Gregory IX, who had appointed him Protector of the Friars Minor in 1228. He is described as a plump, pleasant man who liked to have Friars about him, and was later to add several to his household when he became Pope Alexander IV. The friars were beginning to be in demand in influential places, as they were trusted not to be self-seeking. What St Francis would have thought of this development is perhaps happily unknown.

During his stay in Rome Anthony was asked to preach to the Pope and his Cardinals. They were an impressive audience, drawn from all the nations of the known world. According to the 'Little Flowers of St Francis', among those present were Greeks, Latins, French, Germans, Slavs and English, and others who spoke less well-known languages. Anthony's voice was praised; his learning and holiness delighted the assembled company, and his words became clear to them all, as if each man heard him in his own tongue. The likeness to the miracle of the disciples at Pentecost was not lost on the assembly of eminent clerics. They turned to each other, commenting upon the phenomenon, and the Pope himself hailed Anthony as the 'Ark of the Testament' and 'Armour of the Holy Writ'.

But the principal object was the matter of St Francis's Testament. The friars approached the throne of Peter and put their dilemma. There was much in the Rule they had been given which was obscure, ambiguous, and difficult to understand. It was St Francis's wish that no-one should attempt to interpret the rule for himself. One particular difficulty was his insistence that they should not petition the Pope for papers giving them safe conduct when they were in mission lands, and they emphasised how perplexed and unhappy they were.

What they wanted was a ruling to make these matters clear. They appealed to Gregory – the good friend of St Francis – the man who had been at his elbow when the original Rule was drawn up, and who was well aware of the negotiations that had preceded its approval by the Holy See – to enlighten them about the thinking behind the document.

And they all took the greatest care not to voice the thought which was in everyone's mind; that St Francis was old and sick when he dictated his Will; that the Order had grown around and beyond him, and what was badly needed now was a form of words that would pay lip-service to the veneration in which he was held, while freeing the Order to pursue its present task. Above all, nobody wanted to damage St Francis's reputation.

Gregory's response was a masterpiece of tact. He emphasised that St Francis had drawn up his Testament in all piety and with the best intentions, and that he knew they were anxious to carry out those intentions as far as they were able. But he foresaw endless difficulties and great damage to their consciences if they attempted to interpret the provisions literally. Determinedly and unequivocally he ruled that the Founder's Will was not binding. Francis had drawn it up without consulting anyone, the omission being especially grave in the case of the Provincial ministers who had to administer it personally. He pointed out that in the Order they were all equal; no-one could have jurisdiction over his equals, and St Francis could not legislate for his successors. Once again the Church demonstrated the flexibility and authority of the Papacy, and it must have been with heartfelt sighs of relief that the delegation brought back this ruling from Rome. There is a hint that Anthony might have been offered some sort of sinecure in the Curia. No doubt it was hoped that such an accomplished preacher might always be on hand at the centre of Christendom, but Anthony was already homesick for Padua, his favourite city.

On his way back from Rome, he found a retreat when he

visited St Francis's own mountain of Alverna. The approach, which covered fourteen miles, involved a climb of over three thousand feet, and considering his physical state it was an almost incredible journey. He must have visited the small Friary built to commemorate St Francis's receiving the Stigmata. Today an oratory marks the grotto where Anthony's failing strength was repaired.

Returning to Padua, he spent the winter in writing down his sermons for Feast Days, according to the Roman calendar of the time, though he did not live to complete them. Those from the first of January to the thirtieth of June still exist in the form of notes. He worked on them at the request of his friend the Lord Cardinal of Ostia, the Protector of the Order, although this task had to take second place to his preaching. His fame grew far beyond the city, and as the congregations increased in size and fervour he began to reap the harvest he had sown. There were so many penitents that priests from the surrounding districts had to be brought in to hear their confessions. Public life began to be modelled on Christian principles; bitter enemies forgot their animosity, thieves and prostitutes reformed their lives, and financiers and usurers were so anxious to compensate those they had cheated that they mortgaged their houses and pawned their possessions, asking Anthony to distribute the money to their debtors.

This was a vital service, as they were condemned by law to remain in prison until they had repaid the last farthing. As they were stripped of all their possessions before their incarceration, their case was hopeless, and death was the only relief from utter degradation. When Anthony became aware of their plight, he petitioned Stefano Badoer, the Governor of the city, and succeeded in getting the first bankruptcy law passed on 15th March, 1231, in the following form:

'It is exacted and ordained that no-one henceforth should be held in prison for money debts, past, present or future, if he forfeited his goods. This applies to both debtors and their bondsmen... This statute has been enacted at the insistence of the venerable and blessed Anthony, Confessor of the Order of Friars Minor.'

This final enactment was made as he vowed to preach every day of Lent in all the churches in the city. In the event he was unable to do so, as there were far too many who wished to hear him to be accommodated in any one building, so he took to the open air again, preaching and teaching in spite of his illness. The dropsy from which he suffered made him corpulent; even walking must have tired his swollen limbs, and when he was not giving sermons he was hearing confessions. Sometimes he would get no food or rest until after the sun went down.

A friar told the author of the Primitive Legend that he had heard from Anthony's own lips that during this time he had retired to his cell, having preached all day, and after lying down he felt a sensation in his throat, as if a mighty and malevolent finger and thumb were squeezing his windpipe, on the point of strangling him. He made the sign of the cross, and invoked the help of Our Lady, and woke to find the room 'rosy with the light of heaven'. Of course it would be easy to downgrade this miracle; it may have been a nightmare created by the symptoms of his illness, but we may be sure that the calm which followed when he placed himself in the presence of the Mother of God was heaven sent.

This was another herald of the end, and yet he did not spare himself in his efforts to convert the city he loved, and which loved him. It was not only the debtors who had cause to bless him; he spent his remaining months in preaching to all who wished to hear, giving up his life to proclaim the message of the Gospel.

The death and the burial

During the Lent of 1231, a great wave of piety swept over Padua, and even touched the criminal confraternity. Rigaud, in his early Fourteenth Century life of Anthony, said that in the last decade of the previous century a mendicant friar met a very old man who had once belonged to a gang of robbers living in the woods outside the city, preying on travellers. News of Anthony's eloquence reached the ears of these would-be Robin Hoods and curiosity drove them, suitably disguised, to attend one of his sermons. Overcome by his powerful oratory, they were persuaded to abandon their way of life, and began by making a confession of their misdeeds to the preacher.

He dealt with all twelve miscreants in the same way, exhorting them to keep to their resolution, saying that it was their last chance; if they returned to their former crimes he foresaw that a terrible punishment would overtake them. Having flourished the big stick, he then dangled the carrot – a reward of heavenly life if they would follow in the footsteps of the Saviour.

One or two relapsed, and the elderly penitent witnessed to their miserable demise, but most of those who persevered made peaceful and happy ends. He alone remained, doing the penance Anthony had imposed upon them all, which was to make twelve pilgrimages to the tomb of St Peter in Rome. Having completed his final visit, he was looking forward to the eternal rest he had been promised. Whether Anthony thought that the plunderer of travellers would be better employed as a traveller himself, or that the journeys would occupy his time and keep him out of mischief, we cannot know, but it may well have been this story which has made Anthony the patron of travellers.

Another penitent – a young man, traditionally named Leonardo – had lost his temper with his mother, who seems to have been one of the possessive and nagging variety, and kicked the unfortunate woman. Overcome with remorse, he sought out Anthony and confessed to his sin of extreme anger. Evidently Anthony was not convinced of the youth's sincerity, and to bring the sin home to him said that the offending foot deserved to be cut off. This preyed on Leonardo's mind, and upon his return home he seized an axe and slashed at the unfortunate member. When Anthony heard of this, he was disturbed by such a violent reaction and made his way instantly to the young man's house. Tradition holds that the foot was entirely severed from the leg, and Anthony caused them to be reunited, but it seems reasonable to suppose that the effects might have been less drastic, and some lesser form of healing could have taken place.

While he was kept busy with such incidents, Anthony was still occupied in writing, which must have curtailed his sleep. The round of preaching too went on, and in one of his sermons he refers to the malady that was to kill him, recalling that dropsy, the 'cursed waters', is described in the Book of Numbers as being the disease which 'makes the body swell and the thighs to rot'. He spoke feelingly of the symptoms, particularly 'the burning thirst that could not be quenched'. His disgust with the condition is shown by the comparison he made with a person swollen by lust and greed – lust for pleasure and greed for worldly possessions. He said these conferred a kind of dropsy of the soul, producing an insatiable spiritual thirst.

Verona, Padua's main rival, lay in the bend of the Adige river, dominated by the pink marble amphitheatre where the Romans used to stage gladiatorial combats for up to twenty thousand spectators; and now there was much talk of the plight of the Paduans who were held in Ezzelino's dungeons at Verona. The tyrant Ezzelino was infamous for his terrible cruelty, surpassing that of his predecessors; the torture of his prisoners was commonplace, and in addition they suffered from starvation. The Paduans made several forays to free their fellow-citizens, but without success. Whether Anthony was asked by friends of Count Rizziardo and Matteo Giustiniani, two of the unfortunate captives, or whether he acted on his own initiative is not known; but he never spared himself in granting any request made to him, and he certainly travelled to Verona to petition for their release. In his state of health, it must have been a painful journey; when he reached the city he began by asking the authorities for assistance, and when it seemed that the Governor was powerless to intervene, he tackled Ezzelino himself in his fortress. Sadly, even Anthony's eloquence could not melt that stony heart, and the most he achieved was permission to return to Padua without incurring any of the penalties usually imposed on visitors from that city.

His grief at having to go back empty-handed must have aggravated his physical condition – though perhaps he succeeded better than he knew, for seven months after his death the prisoners were released, and the people of Padua were convinced that their patron's prayers, lovingly invoked, had accounted for the change of policy. Although Ezzelino lived for another twenty years, to massacre a great many more Paduans and flourish in his wickedness, until in 1259, a prisoner at last, he died of wounds inflicted by some of his many enemies.

Overcome by fatigue and disappointment after the failure of his mission, and seeing no end to the devastating enthusiasm of the crowds who followed him everywhere, Anthony eventually wrote to the Provincial who had succeeded him, asking for permission to retire to somewhere quieter, where he could live a life of prayerful contemplation. We may be sure that he drew the attention of his Superior to St Francis's admonition to 'Go away by ourselves, away from the madding crowd, to a lonely place where we can find peace and quiet for body and soul', and he quoted the words of the scriptures: 'Had I but the wings of a dove, I would fly away and be at rest'. Anthony particularly loved doves; while he was preaching on the

Feast of the Purification, in this the last year of his life, when he sang the responsary: 'They offered the Lord for the return of Jesus two turtle-doves or two pigeons', he wondered which of the two species it had been – and two turtle-doves flew out of the roof above his head.

Anthony's letter requesting permission to find a longed-for refuge remained in his cell while he went to ask if there was anyone who could deliver it to the Provincial for him. When a messenger was found, the patron of those who mislay objects was unable to find his own letter. He believed that this was a sign that God wanted him to stay, and resigning himself to the Divine Will, he gave up all thoughts of moving, and told the Warden of the monastery that no communication was to be sent. The days passed, and after enough time had elapsed for a messenger to go and return, Anthony received word from the Provincial, referring to the lost letter and granting his request. From this incident a belief has grown up that Anthony cares particularly for those who correspond by mail.

The place he chose for his retirement was called Camposampiero, where there was a small house of the Friars Minor. Their local landlord was Count Tiso, a good friend of the Order and of Anthony, and the two men had much in common; both were of noble birth, and Count Tiso had also suffered at the hands of Ezzelino. His grandson had been captured by the tyrant's soldiers, and held prisoner in the grim fortress where Anthony had pleaded for the unfortunate victims. Happily, Tiso's grandson was freed after a successful military expedition. Quite near the Friary, there was a large field with many trees in it, belonging to the friendly lord; one in particular, a huge walnut, towered above the rest. It was unusual in that it had six branches spread out under the canopy to form a crown. This phenomenon appealed to Anthony, and he asked Tiso's permission to use the tree as his cell. Tiso did more than grant the request, and apparently wove withies around some stakes with his own hands, making a hut that delighted its new occupant. His faithful companions, Brother Ruggiero and Brother Luke Pelludi, were accommodated in wattle dwellings at the foot of the tree. Today a chapel has been built at this spot, and it contains a picture showing Anthony seated in the branches, preaching to a small crowd assembled on the ground below, all gazing at him attentively except for a toddler playing with a dog in the centre foreground. The occasion is unrecorded in any of the accounts of Anthony's life, and is most probably the invention of the unknown Sixteenth Century artist, but it takes its inspiration from Anthony, and has all the charm of his cult.

Perhaps it was on his way to this haven that Anthony paused at a place where he could see the whole of Padua set out before him. He must have sensed that this was the last time he would see it with mortal eyes, because he gazed at it with such intensity that his companions were aware of the gravity of the moment. He remarked on the beauty of the site and the richness of the fields surrounding it, and added: 'Heaven is about to crown you with a glory still richer and more beautiful.' When they looked back on the incident afterwards, in the light of his death, it seemed that he foresaw the future, when millions would travel from all over the world to enrich the city. Having seen what had happened in Assisi, he rejoiced that Padua too would become a place of pilgrimage.

There is some evidence that he wanted to write a book which might add to the treasury of wisdom in the Church. The proximity of those friars who had taken his dictation on previous occasions argues that he hoped to avail himself of their services once again, but it was not to be. He knew he had not long to live, and was too ill to desire that his ministry should continue, but his hope was that his beloved Padua would share his fame. It was all he had to give, and he gave it freely.

His last hours had a makeshift quality, as if events took everyone by surprise. On Friday, 13th June he awoke in his eyrie in the tree – he seemed to spend most of his time there, no doubt savouring the breeze that swayed the branches – and heard the bell for breakfast sounding in the friary. He hastened to join his brothers at table, but the effort was too much for him; he was seized with an attack of giddiness and fell back, unable to rise. Realising that his legs were too weak to bear him up, the brothers helped him to a couch, where he lay down, but this gave him no relief and he said to Ruggiero, who was attending him: 'Brother, I am a dying man, and I do not wish to give these kind hermits the trouble and expense of a funeral. If you approve the idea, let us go to St Mary's at once.'

Ruggiero tried to dissuade him, as did the members of the hermitage, but they did not succeed in altering his resolution. Eventually they gave way, unable to refuse what might be his last request, and yoked some oxen to a farm-cart, the only transport available. Perhaps they hoped that he would change his mind when he experienced the roughness of the dirt roads, with the ruts baked hard by the sun, but Anthony was determined to reach Padua. Attended by Ruggiero and Luke Pelludi, he began the journey.

On the way they met a friar called Brother Ignoto, who was one of the priests serving the spiritual needs of the Poor Clares' convent at Arcella, near a suburb of Padua called Capodiponte. Ignoto was known to Anthony as a trusted friend, and when he pointed out that as St Mary's was in the middle of the city, full of people coming and going, which would be very tiring for him, he seemed to make some headway against the dying man's obstinacy. Anthony realised that if he did reach the friary, he would be unable to have the peaceful passing he longed for, and the crowds who had made his life a penance with their demands would be dogging his steps as he approached the gates of heaven.

Arcella was only a few minutes away; a cell could be made ready there, and his brothers would assist his passage out of this world. Brother Ignoto's arguments carried the day, and Anthony was carried in to the little friary, to be made as comfortable as possible. We are told that when he found himself face to face with death, he was overcome with fear, becoming a prey to human weakness like lesser men. It must give us great consolation that he shared such feelings with us, but he made his confession, and received absolution and the Viaticum, and that gave him such strength and happiness that he was able to sing in a voice of power and sweetness the hymn to Our Lady, his patron, which begins:

'O gloriosa Domina,
Excelsa supra sidera,
Qui te creavit provide
Lacrasti sacro ubere.'

The song told of Mary's dignity in heaven, and that the singer hoped to have her prayers and protection as he approached the judgement of God, asking that through her divine motherhood she would obtain mercy for him. When Anthony had finished the four stanzas he raised both hands in a gesture of amazement, and his eyes shone with un-earthly brightness, as if he could see something invisible to the rest. Ruggiero, who was supporting him, asked under his breath: 'Do you see anything, Brother?' – and Anthony replied: 'I see my Lord'.

Just then the chaplain came in with the Holy Oil used to administer the sacrament of Extreme Unction. As he made the first movement to anoint him, Anthony, who must already have felt himself to be in the presence of Jesus, said: 'It is not necessary, dear Brother, for I have that ointment already in my heart.' Some of the chroniclers add: 'Nevertheless it is good for me, and I am well pleased', as if they felt that he was lacking in humility. But it is a comfort to think that he had such confidence in the mercy he had begged for, and that his natural anxiety was so wonderfully relieved.

While he received the sacrament, the little community gathered round his bed and recited the seven Penitential Psalms as the liturgy directed. For as long as he was able, Anthony stretched out his arms as if joining his prayers with those of Christ on the cross, and recited with his

Brothers. He did not speak again. For about half an hour his spirit lingered, and then passed into the keeping of the Blessed Trinity.

The Benignitas manuscript tells the story that on the day of Anthony's death, Thomas Gallo, who was Abbot of the Victorine House of St Andrew at Vercelli and Anthony's good friend, was suffering some discomfort from a sore throat. As he was reading in his cell the door opened and Anthony walked in. Thomas Gallo was not at all astonished to see him; his appearance seemed perfectly natural. Anthony said: 'I have come to say good-bye, for I have left the ass at Arcella, and am now hastening to my fatherland.'

Since Abbot Gallo was ignorant of Anthony's death he accepted his words at their face value, thinking he was on his way to Portugal. The apparition then touched his throat, and his discomfort instantly disappeared. Recovering from this pleasant surprise, he found himself alone, and went to the door to find out why Anthony had made his departure so abruptly. He looked into the cloister, but there was no sign of him, so he called to his servants and asked if anyone had seen him, but they denied all knowledge of Anthony's having visited the monastery, and stuck to this conviction in spite of rigorous questioning by their Superior.

He wrote down the whole incident, giving full details of Anthony's appearance and the exact words he had said. Later he discovered that it had taken place at the very day and moment that Anthony had breathed his last. Then he realised that the 'ass' Anthony had mentioned was 'Brother Ass' – the nickname which Francis had given the body, which was familiar to everyone in the Franciscan Order. The 'fatherland' he had spoken about was his home in heaven, which he was now enjoying after his exile on earth. Thomas Gallo was very much moved by this personal visitation, realising that his friend must hold him in great esteem and love, and he could never mention it without tears.

At the time of his death Anthony was thirty-six years old, and by our reckoning in his prime, but owing to the short life expectancy in mediaeval times he was considered to be in late middle-age. In those days there were boy kings, and army commanders in their teens, and many women gave birth when they were scarcely out of childhood; it is no wonder that Pope Gregory IX was revered, since he was eighty-three when he was elected to the Papacy, and his years and memories were rare and valuable.

Grief for Anthony was not due to a premature death, but for the loss of his kind and generous spirit and his great talent. Dominic was dead, Francis was dead; only Anthony had been left, the most prominent of the mendicant friars. In the future there would be Bonaventure and Thomas Aquinas, to dazzle the world with their scholarship, but at that time there was no successor to Anthony on the horizon. He seemed to be irreplaceable.

That was what his passing meant to the academics and to his fellow-preachers. To the people it meant something else. His personality had caught their imagination. They had listened to him in rapt silence when he spoke, and cheered him when he had finished. He was a friend to them all, even while he scolded them and urged them to change their lives. They would miss his way of lifting them up out of their workaday lives, which were nasty, brutish and short, torn by war and filled with backbreaking toil, and his kindness when he assured them of eternal happiness. Anthony had the good news, and he shared it with them. They loved him dearly.

But the friars of Arcella were afraid that such love would be shown in the grisly fashion of the day; Anthony's body would be fought over and dismembered for relics, both by the people and by clerics who should have shown more respect toward one of their number. Even the Poor Clares put in a bid for it, claiming they had a larger chapel than that belonging to the friary and could bury it with greater dignity. That Anthony himself wished to die at St Mary's in the city seemed irrelevant. Everyone wanted his poor swollen body, and the bargaining began as soon as he was cold. The friars had hoped to keep his death a secret until some decision could be reached, but even as he died the children of Padua ran through the streets, as if with some instinctive knowledge, shouting: 'The Saint is dead! Anthony is dead!' – and alerted the city to its loss.

Through a special privilege granted by Pope Gregory IX the friars were entitled to what was called 'free sepulchre', which meant that the parish priest would waive his fee if he said the requiem, and the community had the right of burial in all their monasteries, hermitages and chaplaincies, for themselves but not for outsiders. By this right, the men at St Mary's claimed his body since that was Anthony's usual abode, but the Abbess of the Poor Clares laid claim to his remains since her chaplains were Franciscans and he died in the chaplaincy. She rallied her forces, which included many of the most influential civic dignitaries; the Order was popular with fashionable ladies, and some of their members were very well-connected.

Rumours were spreading of miracles performed in the vicinity of the death chamber, and people began to crowd into it to say their farewells. Some sort of order had to be kept so that they could file in and take their last look at the face now so serene. The common people took the friars' side in the argument, if only to spite their betters. Then the Bishop and his Canons became involved; ignoring the advice they were given, that the nuns had the better case, they wrote to the Governor, saying he should give free passage to the friars to take Anthony's body to St Mary's. To do this they would have had to negotiate the river Bacchiglione – but they were not given the chance. People from the city began to flock to the suburb, determined to take part in the dispute. The friars mounted guard over their late brother and recited the Office of the Dead, but were interrupted by a rowdy gang of newcomers who wrenched the door of the chaplaincy off its hinges and burst in upon the tearful scene.

Things were no better next morning, when the news had spread through the surrounding countryside. Crowds arrived on foot, on horseback and crammed into wagons, all converging on the tiny cell. Those who managed to get inside touched the body with anything they had with them, knowing that it would instantly become a precious relic. Those outside despaired of getting any closer and handed in rings, necklaces, belts, coins or keys to be touched by anyone fortunate enough to gain admittance. Some, still more ingenious, suspended the objects on poles or fishing rods which they pushed in through the windows, hoping that somebody would take pity on their deprivation, touch the body with the talisman and return it, hallowed by this contact.

To prevent further sacrilege the chaplains decided to give the body provisional burial, and enclosed it in a simple wooden coffin. They chose the afternoon hour generally dedicated to the siesta, hoping that as few people as possible should know of this move, but it proved impossible to do such a thing unobserved, and a great cry went up: 'They have taken away the body!' This was the signal for a riot to break out. The windows were broken and the remaining doors smashed down by the most reckless mourners, desperate to gain access. The intruders would not move until the coffin had been dug up and beaten with sticks to prove it was not empty. Before we pride ourselves that the world is more civilised today, we must remember that rioting did not end with the Middle Ages. Comparable desecration has occurred at sectarian funerals in our own day, and are not confined to any one country or religion. Sadly, pious fervour can turn easily to violence, and despite everyone's best endeavours that is what happened at Arcella, the scene of Anthony's death.

Later, on the night of Saturday, 14th June, the Provincial Minister of the Order of Friars Minor arrived to watch over its most famous son. He refused to commit himself to any course of action until he had seen the Governor of Padua, Stefano Badoer, who had the power of the secular arm to enforce his decision – though he was no more anxious than anyone else to assume the responsibility of making one. Since mob rule seemed likely to take over, the

126

Governor appointed a military guard over the chaplaincy and read out an order that a heavy fine should be imposed on anyone molesting the friars, then waited to see if this would have any effect.

The friars were used to going without sleep, but they were suffering bereavement of the man who had been a friend to them all, though he had spent only a few hours in their company. The feelings of Brother Ruggiero and Brother Luke Pelludi may be imagined, for their loss was incalculable. For years they had been close to Anthony, sharing hardship and deprivation, but also the deep joy in all created things which is part of the Franciscan way of life. They were glad that his sufferings were over, and they knew one so holy would find no bar on the gate of heaven, but their own sorrow at parting with such a wonderful companion must have weighed them down. At the centre of the tumult, they remained mute, overcome by grief.

At last someone thought to ask them what Anthony's own wishes had been. They replied that he had made known to them his desire to rest in St Mary's at Padua, and but for the chance encounter with Brother Ignoto he would surely have died there. Word was carried to the Bishop, who ordered that the funeral should take place on the following day, Sunday the 15th. The Governor and the Provincial Minister were informed so that they could make all the civil and liturgical arrangements.

It was realised that the cortege would have to pass over the river separating Capodiponte from the city. There was only one bridge, and the way on to it would swiftly become choked by the hordes who wished to join the funeral procession. After examining the problem, it was decided that another bridge should be built out of barges, from a point opposite the chaplaincy, higher upstream than the existing bridge. A team of men were set the task of constructing it during the night of 14th/15th June – one of the shortest of the year. They succeeded in making it ready by the appointed time, only to have their handiwork hacked to pieces by the men of Capodiponte in an orgy of destruction, furious at being deprived of their saint – for in their hearts he had already been canonised.

People in the city heard of these events and rushed to the scene in their turn, anxious to join in the struggle on their own behalf. The friars of St Mary's lamented the way things had turned out, and blamed themselves for the destruction that had overtaken the city, while the Poor Ladies wept to think that they too had a share in provoking such violence. The Governor showed his mettle by calling a meeting of all the citizens, and informed them that the men who had destroyed the bridge would not be allowed to return to the scene of their crime, on pain of forfeiture of their estates, which indicates that some of the miscreants at least were well-to-do, and this cooled their ardour for the fight considerably.

The Bishop and his retinue led the way to the chaplaincy, which was still showing signs of its siege. The coffin was brought forth and the Governor and some of the highest-ranking officials in the State, together with able-bodied men from all the noblest houses, took turns in carrying the precious freight. Singing of the pain of their loss and the triumph of Anthony's rebirth into eternal life, and accompanied by a vast concourse carrying flaming torches, they negotiated the original bridge without the anticipated difficulty. The procession reached St Mary's with no mishaps, which was a kind of miracle in itself; the Bishop sang the Requiem, and Anthony's body was interred in a fine stone sarcophagus.

At first the miracles were only rumours. A story was told of one of the Poor Ladies, a Sister Olivia, who had kissed the hand of the dead saint and petitioned to be allowed to have her Purgatory in this world rather than the next. On the following day she was at supper in the community when she was seized with such pain that she cried aloud, and was taken to the Infirmary, where she continued to suffer. She remembered that she had a piece of Anthony's habit, snipped off one day while he was preaching, and when she applied it to the afflicted place the pain ceased immediately. Perhaps this was not very remarkable in itself, but it was the herald of many more extraordinary happenings. People began to keep a tally – sixteen cripples cured, and two epileptics were listed – and the totals kept on mounting all the time. The church at St Mary's was crammed with petitions, and the sick laid out in rows on the Piazza.

It became the custom to bring candles to the tomb; no doubt this was the origin of the practice of lighting candles at the foot of Anthony's statues, which still continues everywhere. In the heady days just after his burial, the candles were of fantastic size and shape. Some were so huge, they were carried by ox-wagon, and needed as many as sixteen strong men to haul them into the church; others had to remain outside because they were so bulky. Many were decorated with pictures of books, a reference to Anthony's learning, and some were fashioned like lilies; this was the first sign of Anthony's connection with the flower that denotes purity of life.

All this meant that a cry arose for his canonisation by popular acclaim. The blind saw, the deaf heard, the lame walked, the dumb spoke his praises. Faith accounted for many of the miracles, but unbelievers too were converted. The news of the wonders at Padua spread rapidly; crowds came from all parts of Italy and beyond to share in the cornucopia of divine grace that was poured forth.

Within a month a deputation of the most considerable citizens went to Rome, petitioning the Holy See to investigate Anthony's cause. The Bishop of Padua and the Priors of the Dominicans and Benedictines were commissioned to look into the 'alleged miracles'. Witnesses were subjected to most careful scrutiny; notes were taken of their names and ages, their maladies, and their social standing, if any. How, when and where the cures were performed was taken into account, and all those who had been present were questioned. Forty-six miracles passed the test. The three commissioners sent their findings to the Curia, with letters from the Bishop and the Governor of Padua; nobles and citizens, and the Master and scholars of the University added their own petitions and testimonies.

Things were hurried along when Cardinal Ottone of Monferrato and the Bishop Elect of Palestrina, both independent witnesses, passed through Padua on a visit to settle disagreements in the Lombard towns. Becoming interested in the inquiry, they wrote to the Curia, adding their voices to the rest. Pope Gregory IX convoked a consistory headed by Lord John, Bishop of Sabina, an influential cleric who, the previous year, had been entrusted with the reconciliation between Frederick II and the Holy See. For the people of Padua it was an exhilarating but testing time. Realising that any more unrest would spoil their chances of having a saint of their own, they behaved in an exemplary fashion. The amendment in their lives, which had begun when Anthony was with them, was resumed. Piety flourished like the trees of the forest he loved and mentioned so often in his sermons. If the people were impatient with the Vatican, they kept it to themselves.

Then one night the Supreme Pontiff had a dream, in which he was surrounded by his Cardinals, all wearing sumptuous vestments. They had gathered to consecrate a new altar, and he asked where the relics were, which had to be incorporated? On being told there were none, he demanded that new relics should be sought. By the altar was a body awaiting burial, and he suggested that this should be the source of the relics. The body, when handled carefully, was found to be incorrupt. Since Anthony's cause had been so much on his mind, he took the dream to mean that it should be proved justified – and the waiting was over. The Cardinal Archbishop of Sabina reported favourably, the last obstacle was swept away, and Padua planned a festival that would put all others to shame.

The making of a saint

Not many ordinary Paduans would have been able to travel over two hundred miles south to the city of Spoleto in Umbria, though some would certainly have made the pilgrimage.

Spoleto is built on hills, and when the Pope took possession of the town in 1213 it made a suitable retreat from the oppressive heat of the Roman summer. It had been largely devastated by Frederick II's father, Barbarossa, in the middle of the Twelfth Century, apart from a Roman amphitheatre and several triumphal arches which defied even his power to flatten them. In reparation, he gave its Cathedral a splendid mosaic floor, but there were greater benefits to be acquired from allegiance to the Holy See, and the citizens were happy to be within its jurisdiction. Many churches and monasteries owe their foundation to this time. A few miles away, the forest of Monteluco had provided one of St Francis's retreats, and in its peaceful depths Anthony too was commemorated by a grotto shrine.

A cosmopolitan crowd must have gathered in the Cathedral of Spoleto and on the pleasant piazza outside with its hanging gardens, as Gregory IX prepared, slightly less than a year after Anthony's death, to place him in the Calendar. The papal court, with a full complement of cardinals, archbishops, bishops, and heads of religious orders, was present in strength. The nobility were gathered to see one of their number honoured, together with a vast crowd of ordinary men and women. The people of Spoleto, mostly fruit and vegetable growers and vineyard workers, gave their support to one who was known to be a champion of the poor.

The conclusion of the consistory was made known, and the forty-six miracles that had been testified before it were

read out in detail. Anthony was rich in the other require-
ment that the Church demands of its saints – sanctity of life
– and this was affirmed by the members who had investi-
gated his cause. The Holy Father himself then rose and
proclaimed to the glittering assembly that Anthony was
henceforth to be known as St Anthony, and that his feast
would be kept each year on the day of his death, 13th June.

The church bells rang out, and their clangour echoed
wherever the devotion to the new saint had been established; then everyone united in singing the Te Deum. Carried away by the emotion that the ceremony had engendered,
Gregory IX broke spontaneously into the Antiphon: 'O
Doctor optime', from the breviary. This was the greeting
normally reserved for the official doctors of the Church, of
whom there were at that time only four, all from the ages
of antiquity. Nevertheless the Pope saluted the Saint: 'O
excellent Doctor, light of Holy Church, blessed Anthony!
Lover of God's law, pray for us to the Son of God.'

So began the cult of St Anthony, venerated first in the
liturgy of the Franciscan Order, and very soon throughout
the world. In the liturgical reforms of 1570, Pope Pius V
removed Anthony from the Calendar, but this demotion of
their favourite saint caused such an outcry amongst the
faithful that his feast was restored by Sextus V, who extended it to the Church Universal in the bull 'Immensa',
dated 14th January 1586, describing him as 'a man of
exceptional sanctity and endowed with divine wisdom'.
Perhaps it is not entirely coincidental that Sextus was no
mean preacher himself, a professor of theology, and a
Franciscan.

The original declaration on 30th May 1232, was followed a few days later by a papal bull, announcing the
canonisation to the whole world:

'Gregory, Bishop, Servant of the Servants of God, to the
venerable brethren, the archbishops and bishops, and to the
beloved sons, abbots, priors, and other prelates of the
Church; health and apostolic benediction. The Lord says
through the prophets: "I will give you to all the people for

praise and glory and honour," and promises through himself that the just will shine forth like the sun in the sight of God. Therefore it is an act of piety and justice that those whom God crowns and honours in heaven, because of their merit and holiness, we should honour on earth by our prayers and veneration. We more truly praise God in them because his praise and glory is seen forever in his saints. He shows his power most wonderfully, and his care for the work of our salvation, by giving his faithful ones here on earth glory, by performing signs and wonders. In this way he nullifies the evil done by heresy, and enhances the true Catholic belief.

'So the faithful turn from being lukewarm, and are roused to show enthusiasm for good works; unbelievers are led from the darkness and blindness in which they dwell, and back to the right way; and even Jews and pagans are enlightened by Christ, who is the Light, the Way, the Truth and the Life.

'Wherefore, beloved sons, we give thanks (if not as much as we should, at least as much as we can) to the source of all Grace, that in our days he has visibly worked new signs and revealed the might of his power, giving new glory to those on earth who strengthen the Catholic faith by their wholehearted service, their words and their deeds. Among these is the Blessed Anthony of holy memory, of the Order of Friars Minor, who while on earth possessed great gifts, and now that he is living in heaven has shown us his glory by many miracles, which are signs of his great holiness.

'Although it is sufficient to show perseverance to the end in order to be accepted as a saint in the Church Triumphant (for the Lord says: "Be faithful unto death, and I will give you the crown of life") nevertheless to be considered a saint by those who belong to the Church here on earth two things are necessary – virtues and miracles. These bear witness to each other, since neither is sufficient on its own to prove anyone's holiness. But when genuine virtue is present and miracles follow, we do see those signs of holiness that lead us to venerate the possessor.

133

'By the advice of our brethren the cardinals, and all the prelates dwelling at the papal court, we have decreed to enrol in the catalogue of the saints Anthony, who after his earthly life has merited to be with Christ in heaven. We would seem to begrudge the honour due to him if we left him without the honour with which God has seen fit to endow him. Because the Gospel teaches us that men do not light a lamp to cover it up but put it on a lamp stand, so as to give light to everyone in the house, we see the lamp of this saint shining so brilliantly that by God's grace we too should display it on a lamp stand.

'We beseech you, admonish you earnestly, and bid you through this communication, to encourage the faithful to honour him for their own salvation, to celebrate his feast and cause it to be held on the thirteenth day of June each year, that God will be moved by his prayers to grant us grace in this present life, and glory in the life to come. Wishing further that the tomb of this great Confessor, who through his miracles has already shed the reflection of his glory on the Church, be suitably honoured and visited, we, confiding in the mercy of God and the authority of the Blessed Apostles Peter and Paul, grant to all who are re-pentant and have made their confession, and reverently visit it on his feast or within the octave, an indulgence of one year of the penance they have imposed on them. Given at Spoleto on the eleventh of June, in the sixth year of our pontificate.'

Several of the posthumous miracles confirmed by the Bishop of Padua took place in the city, or the surrounding countryside. One tale is told of a convent servant called Peter, whose tongue was malformed so that he was dumb; he was also deaf and simple-minded. Peter had a vision that encouraged him to turn to St Anthony for help, but being unaware that Anthony had died, he went hopefully around the convent, looking for him. Failing to find him, he went out and searched in the fields, but to no avail. Then the vision returned to comfort him in his disappointment, and urged him to persevere. He came to the church of St Anthony and in his own unorthodox fashion prayed all through the night. About nine o'clock in the morning he was overtaken by a fit of trembling and bathed in sweat. A divine light sprang up around him, and he was no longer tongue-tied. He could hear and speak, though at first no-one could understand him because he used an unfamiliar language; only a few basic words were intelligible. After a time he astonished those who knew him by talking of things no-one could possibly have taught him, and people gathered to listen to his words of wisdom. They praised God for his new-found erudition – and they called him Anthony.

Another story tells of a leper who came to Padua, seeking for a cure through St Anthony's prayers. A horseman he met along the road made fun of his quest, saying that if he were cured, he would take on the leprosy himself. The leper lay down beside the saint's tomb and prayed devoutly. It was very late, and he fell asleep, dreaming that St Anthony came to him and told him he was cured. The dream figure ordered him to go to the man who had mocked the idea of his being cleansed, and take him the rattle which, as a leper, he had been bound to carry everywhere, in order to warn people of his approach. The leper did as he was asked, and found the horseman, who had already received some marks of the disease, and told him of his cure. The afflicted man, much moved by the reversal of their situations, vowed never to make fun of the cult of St Anthony again – and later recovered his health.

From time to time, sceptics made fun of the popular cult. One man went so far as to make an elaborate attempt to trick people into thinking he was blind. He bound his eyes with a bloodstained bandage, and called out: 'Blessed Anthony has restored my sight.' When his companions tore off the bandage, the man was horrified to discover that he had indeed been struck by blindness. He confessed what had happened, and he and his awe-struck companions began to pray, whereupon he found that he could see again.

From these stories we see some definite traits emerging. St Anthony was often said to have appeared in dreams.

Devotees will recognise in this his delicacy of touch, since in sleep he could appear without frightening anyone. Another characteristic was that, having once turned the tables on people who mocked him or teased his followers, he did not make their discomfiture permanent.

This is also apparent in the story of a man consulting a priest who dabbled in necromancy; together they summoned up demons, hoping to learn some arcane secrets. The man stood in the middle of a circle, and the demons gathered around the circumference, making a loud noise. Gruesome details were added; it was said that they tore out the man's tongue and his eyeballs. Terrified and contrite, he called on St Anthony and begged to be received into the Convent of the Friars Minor, where he spent many days and nights. Then one morning when Mass was being celebrated and the friars were singing the Benedictus at the elevation, he saw the sacrament held aloft. The people around him were astounded, and began to pray to St Anthony that his tongue too should be restored. When the words: 'Dona nobis pacem' were reached in the Agnus Dei, his tongue and speech returned, through the Saint's intercession.

Work had begun on St Anthony's Basilica as soon as he was canonised, during the transition between the simple Romanesque style and the intricacy of the Gothic, and continued for at least a hundred years. It was not until 1263 that the transept was considered ready to receive the relics of the Saint. Then the future St Bonaventure, Doctor of the Church, was present. He was only ten years old when St Anthony died, but he knew people who had known him, and formed a great devotion to him. He was also familiar with many of the territories famed for their connection with St Anthony – Spain and Portugal, and many of the towns in France where he had preached. When Bonaventure became Minister General of the Order of Friars Minor, he revised the Rule, laying a restriction on the pictures that could be displayed in Franciscan churches. The only ones allowed were of the Crucifixion, the Virgin Mary, St Francis and St

Anthony of Padua; and he declared this at Narbonne in 1260.

Three years later, at the translation of the relics, he said in his address: 'Blessed Anthony desired the Order of Friars Minor to beg for alms and to possess nothing under heaven.' He recalled that it was the example of St Francis which made Anthony follow the way of poverty in his footsteps, and that he had always been a renowned imitator of the founder. It was the sight of the relics of the Five Promartyrs of the Franciscan Order at Coimbra that had inspired him to travel into pagan lands, in the hope that he too would shed his blood for Christ, and although he was thwarted in this intention, he might well have achieved martyrdom by desire. Bonaventure went on to say that St Anthony had shown humility by begging the Guardian of the Hermitage at Monte Paolo, where he acted as priest to six of the brothers, to allow him to sweep floors and wash dishes, to make up for his failure to die by the sword in Morocco. This emphasis on the Saint's humility was no doubt to remind members of the Order, now so much more powerful, of the purity of the original interpretation of the Rule.

Then he opened the coffin and found that while it contained dust and bones, as was to he expected so long after death, the Saint's tongue remained just as it had been in life. Bonaventure kissed it fervently, exclaiming: 'O Blessed tongue, you have always praised the Lord and led others to praise him. Now we can see clearly how great indeed have been your merits before God.' A special reliquary was made for it by a pupil of Ghiberti, the celebrated goldsmith. During the French Revolutionary wars the French troops were anxious to steal this treasure, but the inhabitants of Padua hastily collected enough money to ransom the precious relic of their beloved Saint.

The General Chapter of 1310 was held at Padua, and the Friars placed the relics in an especially built chapel. Forty years later the Basilica was completed, and the relics found another resting-place. Cardinal Guy de Montfort, the Papal

Legate, suffered what he believed to be a mortal illness when he was at Cuges, at the mouth of the Rhone. He appealed to St Anthony, who responded by obtaining his cure. In gratitude he made a pilgrimage to Padua, donating a magnificent reliquary of silver which was placed in the shrine on which the altar rests, and he gained the skull of the Saint for Cuges, where it is venerated.

About 1630 the Chapel of the Saint's tomb was enriched by nine marble sculptures of the Venetian School; just one of many Renaissance projects to give honour to the Saint. Inspired by his life, painters too, including Titian and Donatello, did some of their best work. A fresco of St Anthony was painted by Giotto – a member of the Third Order of St Francis. Giotto's life spanned sixty-one years from 1276, so he painted his likeness of the Saint within a hundred years of his death. The face is depicted as calm and dignified; a young man, tonsured, and without a beard. His eyes and mouth have the faintest of smiles. Clients of St Anthony will insist on the truth of this representation.

The relics found their final resting-place in 1745, deposited in their present site by the Cardinal Bishop of Padua. Disaster threatened when the Basilica was badly damaged by fire, but the altar escaped unscathed. The citizens of Padua believed that it was through St Anthony's good offices that no-one was hurt in the hurricane of 1756. The crowded City Hall had its roof blown off, and there was extensive damage but no casualties. The Bishop gave thanks, not only organising processions to the altar on three successive days, but by caring for those who had been made destitute on account of the storm.

This was not the first time that the Paduans had cause to bless St Anthony for their preservation from disaster. When the city was occupied by the tyrant Ezzelino di Romagna – who had figured in St Anthony's story earlier – a siege was mounted by the Papal Legate to oust him, causing the citizens still more hardship in addition to the trials already created by his tyranny. The Warden of the Friars Minor prayed at St Anthony's tomb for relief from their suffering, and heard a voice say: 'Fra Bartolemeo, do not be sorrow-ful or afraid; on the Octave of my Feast freedom will be restored to the city of Padua, which will enjoy pristine safety.' Many friars heard the voice as they held vigil in the chapel, and testified to it – and indeed the city was freed on 20th June 1256. When the news of these reassuring words circulated through Padua, the people insisted on keeping the Octave with as much solemnity as they did the Feast, and they continued to observe both occasions for many years.

The friar in question was not alone in finding solace at St Anthony's tomb. A certain Brother Cambio came from Romagna to request St Anthony's help in curing a rupture. As usual, the crowds were closely massed round the sar-cophagus, and he could not pass between the columns around it, but he reached out as far as he could and briefly managed to touch it. When he placed the hand which had made the contact on the place where he felt pain, the rupture, which had gaped open, was as firm as his fore-head. With true Franciscan abandon he danced with joy, and expressed his delight similarly whenever he told the story, announcing: 'To your honour and glory, glorious St Anthony – not so long ago I couldn't have done this!'

A young mother who was working in the fields had a baby girl, who fell into a ditch between two rows of vines and drowned. She promised to put a candle fashioned in the shape of her daughter upon St Anthony's tomb, if she was restored to life. When the child revived, she made good her promise. Another woman, also a field-worker, was called Vita. She wanted to visit the tomb, but had to stay behind to scare sparrows from the millet which was almost ready to harvest. Such was her desire to honour the Saint, she made a bargain with him that she would visit the tomb nine times if he would keep the birds at bay. As she uttered these words, a great flock of sparrows rose up and flew away, never to return.

St Anthony seems to have a special power over the weather, and there are at least two storm stories. One happened in the Venetian lagoon, when a group of people were sailing near San Giorgio in Alga (St George-in-the-Seaweed). The sky grew black, a great tempest threw them off course, and they were lost without any means of navigation. A priest on board persuaded them to confess, which they were very glad to do, feeling themselves to be in danger of death. The priest gave them absolution, and they appealed to St Anthony to save them. They drifted on at the mercy of the wind and rain, but it seemed to them that a light appeared in the sky and went before them until they found themselves near St Mark's, where the light disappeared, amid rejoicing from the company.

The second storm tale is about a relative of St Anthony himself – in some accounts his nephew – who, when quite a child, went with some older companions for a sailing trip. As the weather worsened the older children swam for their lives, but the boy was unable to follow their example and sank like a stone into the turbulent water. His mother searched the shore, asking some fishermen to help her, and they eventually found the lad's body, entangled in their nets. Although they did their best to resuscitate him, it was to no avail. The mother refused to have her son buried, and invoked St Anthony's prayers, saying she would give the boy to the Friars Minor if he recovered. After three days, he rose from the dead in the presence of many bystanders, and when he grew up he did indeed become a member of the Order; an exemplary friar, he never tired of telling his story to anyone who cared to listen.

Another child, no less than the Queen of Aragon's daughter, was raised from the dead due to the Saint's intercession, but she had been enjoying the delights of heaven and was not in the least grateful for his good offices, saying to her relatives: 'The Lord has promised me that I shall only abide with you for fifteen days.'

From Sapei in Portugal comes the story of the woman who had a wicked and licentious husband. She was so miserable, she attempted to hang herself, and was about to put her head in the noose when she heard knocking at the door. She hid the rope and opened the door, and there were two Friars Minor, who said they had come from a far country, and were called Anthony and Francis. As she had a great devotion to St Anthony and St Francis, she asked them in, and they spoke so comfortingly to her as she prepared a meal for them that she decided not to kill herself after all. They parted for the night, and the friars appeared to the woman's husband, who was away from home, telling him they were St Francis and St Anthony, and saying that he must be converted and be faithful to his wife or he would die in three days and go to hell. 'You have already driven your wife to attempt suicide,' they said, 'and if we hadn't come she would have hanged herself. If you don't believe us, ask her to show you the rope she was going to use.'

In the morning he returned to his house, where his wife was amazed to find the friars gone, even though the doors were locked. When her husband asked her kindly where the rope was, she was too astonished to reply, and he went on to say how much they owed the Saints for their delivery from evil. He explained his vision, and she described hers; he asked her to forgive him, and they lived on in harmony, giving thanks to God and St Anthony and St Francis, and doing many good works.

It was not only in his own country or in Padua that St Anthony made his prayers available, neither did they diminish as time went by. A woman visited the Franciscan chapel in Bologna on Tuesday, every week for nine weeks, to take communion and ask that she should become pregnant. Her hopes were realised, but when the baby was born it was terribly deformed. Refusing to believe that St Anthony had disappointed her, she took the child and exposed it on his altar. Even as she watched, it took on the appearance of great beauty. Word went round, and tradition has it that this was the origin of the devotion of the Nine Tuesdays, on which St Anthony's clients hear Mass, and light candles before the Saint's statue, seeking specific favours. Later, some people attended for thirteen Tuesdays, in honour of the date of St Anthony's death.

As recently as 1892 a woman of Toulon, Louise Bouffier, wanted to become a Carmelite but had to care for her parents, who were infirm, so she earned the family's living by running a shop. One morning when she went to open up, she could not budge the lock of the shop door. A locksmith she called in was no more successful, despite trying keys for almost an hour. Eventually he said he would fetch his tools and break in. As Louise Bouffier awaited his return she was inspired to say: 'I promise some bread for St Anthony's poor if he will open the door without breaking the lock.' The locksmith arrived, and she begged him to try with the key just once more. He agreed, and the very next key he used opened the door. From this incident grew the custom of offering St Anthony bread for the poor in exchange for favours received. There are several stories of children, who had received special cures from St Anthony; after their parents had successfully interceded for their lives, they left their children's weight in corn as a donation to charity.

Although St Anthony's own letter to his Provincial is the origin of his being the patron of the mail, this was not all. In 1729 his namesake Antonio, surnamed Dante, left Spain for South America to set up a business in Lima, Peru. His wife being left at home, she became very alarmed as the months went by without even a line from him, although she had written to him many times. She went to the church of St Francis in Oviedo, which had a chapel with a statue of St Anthony; putting a letter into its hands, she asked the Saint to see that her husband received it. Next day she returned and saw that what appeared to be her letter was still there. In her disappointment, she reproached the Saint.

As she did so, the Brother Sacristan came by and said he had tried to remove the letter, but had failed. Señora Dante tried, and found it slipped easily into her hand, and a shower of gold coins rained down from the sleeves of the statue. The letter proved to be from her husband, saying that he had received her letter with great joy because, not having heard from her, he had believed her to be dead. Her letter had come to him through a Franciscan friar, and he was sending the reply by the same messenger, with three hundred gold coins for her support. He also recommended her to his patron, St Anthony. This letter was kept at Oviedo, and shown as proof of the miracle.

St Anthony is also the Patron of his home city, Lisbon. During the great earthquake of 1775, the city was reduced to heaps of rubble. St Anthony's altar was found amongst the ruins, and a young man who had taken refuge at its foot was miraculously preserved. One of the first things to be repaired was the Saint's shrine. The children wanted to help, so they made small shrines of their own out of whatever material came to hand, and asked for money, rather in the way English children show a home-made Guy Fawkes in memory of the Gunpowder Plot. Even after the shrine was restored, they went on with the custom, and the money was spent – as it is in England – on fireworks to be set off on the Feast.

St Anthony is remembered in Rome for a miracle that occurred in 1830. When a little boy fell from a third-floor window, his mother found him quite unharmed in the street below, and he claimed that he had been caught by a monk, who afterwards disappeared. They went to a Franciscan church to give thanks, and when the boy saw a picture of St Anthony, he said he recognised his rescuer.

In Coimbra, his statue is robed as a Canon Regular, and he is called St Anthony of Lisbon. In the parish church of the city, he is dressed as an acolyte to commemorate the office he performed there. It is not perhaps so obvious why in Brazil he wears the uniform of an army officer, and the Friars Minor receive the salary appropriate to his rank. Portugal also gave him military honours when in 1688 he was enlisted as a private soldier in the Lagos Regiment. Five years later, due to 'good services and miracles performed for the benefit of our troops' he was promoted to Captain.

Many of the Popes praised him in the highest terms. He might well have echoed St Francis by calling Gregory IX

143

'my Pope', since when Gregory heard Anthony preach he called him 'the Ark of the Testament', and at the ceremony of canonisation said he was 'full of merits and resplendent with miracles'. Sixtus IV, who built the Sistine Chapel but did nothing to extend the moral authority of the Papacy, nevertheless thought highly of St Anthony, describing him as 'a most brilliant star which rose from on high to illuminate the world'. This tribute was given two and a half centuries after his death.

When Sixtus V extended St Anthony's Feast to the whole Church on 14th January 1586, he said he was 'a man of exceptional sanctity, and endowed with divine wisdom'. At the turn of the Nineteenth Century, Leo XIII, who called himself 'the prisoner of the Vatican' and was Supreme Pontiff for thirty-four years, fighting hard against the heresies and agnosticism of his day, affirmed that St Anthony was 'Saint of the whole world, who shone like a star in the house of God to disperse the darkness of errors, while by his eloquence he revealed the scriptures, solved controversies and clarified doubts'.

On the seven hundredth anniversary of his death in 1931, Pius XI led the celebrations, saying that 'St Anthony by the means of his eloquence caused in his day the purity of the Gospel to revive; he combated heretics and recalled the erring to the bosom of Mother Church'. As the world breathed more freely after the end of the Second World War, his successor, Pius XII, gave him an even higher honour. In 1946, on the Feast of the Promartyrs of the Franciscan Order, 16th January – a day especially chosen because it meant so much in the life of the Saint – the Pope proclaimed him a Doctor of the Universal Church. The Apostolic Letter announcing the elevation, 'Exulta Luisitania Felix' – 'Be glad, fruitful Portugal' – went on: 'O faithful Padua, be glad! – for you have borne unto earth and heaven a hero, not unequal to the gleaming sun, glowing with holiness of life and renown for miracles, as well as the radiant splendour of heavenly doctrine, who has illuminated the whole world and even yet sheds upon it a vivid light.' Then he mentioned the great wave of enthusiasm for the seven hundredth anniversary celebrations, and the flood of requests from the Orders and Universities pressing for further recognition for the Saint who combined learning with great popular appeal. The cause had lain dormant through the upheaval of the war, but now he was judged by representatives of the Sacred Congregation to have the trinity of requirements for a Doctorate – outstanding sanctity of life, eminent divine learning, and the declaration of the Supreme Pontiff.

That he deserved his new eminence was obvious from those of his teachings which have come down to us. The doctrines he expounds in his sermons have, one by one, been defined by the Church. As recently as 1950, the same Pius XII called him as a witness when defining the doctrine of the Assumption of Our Lady into heaven. Anthony also preached on the Kingship of Christ, the veneration of the Sacred Heart, the devotion to the Holy Name, Mary's Immaculate Conception, her special relationship with the human race as Co-Redemptrix and Mediatrix, and the Primacy and Infallibility of Peter and his successors.

Nowhere was the news welcomed more warmly than in America, the continent that had lain undiscovered to the west of Anthony's native country, and Portuguese sailors had been among the first to glimpse its shores. There was a great seminar of distinguished clerics and laymen in Washington, all adding their tributes. Cardinal Cushing, archbishop of Boston, summed up the general feeling when he said: 'The things that captured St Anthony, and with which he captured others were – first, the evangelical spirit, and second, the spirit of poverty.'

But there were among the common people those who felt the title 'Doctor of the Church' distanced them from their beloved Saint, and in South America they refused to accept his elevation. His ordinary devotees begged his prayers out of the small desperations of their workaday lives; to them he is still the guardian of letters and retriever of lost objects; he, who spent so much of his time making long journeys, is the patron of travellers. He protects priests, children, engaged couples and pregnant women, and is a saviour in times of famine, war and pestilence.

Everywhere he went, his shrines are places of pilgrimage. There is a monastery built in 1656 on the site of the little hermitage at Oliveres, the place where he first took the Franciscan habit, given to the Order by Queen Urraca of Portugal. It was completely destroyed by fire in 1851, but the church and its sacristy were saved, together with their commemorative tablets and frescoes. Near the site of the cell which is reputed to be St Anthony's, there is a splendid view of the surrounding countryside, a wide expanse of hills and valleys, edged like an amphitheatre by mountains, with distant views of the sea.

All across France and Italy there are grottoes and chapels and churches where he is remembered. Every place he visited, to preach or to contemplate, has its shrine, with its inevitable store of commemorative tablets for favours received. The Basilica in Padua is always crowded with pilgrims who wonder at the works of art and the reliquaries in the treasure house, and kneel at the tomb of the Saint, magnificent with statues and giant candles. It is a very far cry from his own life of poverty, and as with all Franciscan saints, one wonders if such opulence is appropriate. But in other places, far removed from centres of organised pilgrimage, it is possible to see what he saw, and pray where he prayed, and his presence spans the centuries. He has been with us for eight hundred years, and he is with us today.

In obscure corners of dusty grey cathedrals, or bright modern parish churches with wall-to-wall carpeting and amplification facilities, you are here with the lily, the child and the book, always trusted, always accessible. You light a candle of faith in our hearts – dear St Anthony, friend of all the world.

The prayers and praises

The following prayers are traditionally attributed to St Anthony

A prayer for humility

Christ Jesus,
You conquered the pride of the evil one
By the humility of your incarnation:
Grant also to us
To shatter the chains of pride and arrogance
By the humility of our heart,
So we may be worthy of the gift of your glory
With your help, who are blessed from age to age.
Amen.

A prayer before preaching

Light of the World, Infinite God, Father Eternal, Giver of Wisdom and Knowledge, most holy and ineffable Dispenser of Spiritual Grace, who hast made known all things from the beginning, who hast made darkness and light; guide my hand and touch my lips that they may be like a sharp sword to set forth Thy Truth. Make, O Lord, my tongue like a swift arrow to declare Thy marvellous works. Send forth, O God, Thy Holy Spirit into my heart that I may perceive; into my mind that I may remember; into my soul that I may meditate. Inspire me to speak with piety, holiness, tenderness and mercy. Teach, guide and direct my thoughts and senses from the beginning to the end. May Thy grace ever help and correct me, and may I be strengthened now with wisdom from on high, for Thy infinite mercy's sake. Amen.

A prayer after preaching

O Lord, only in thy name will I cast my net, because each time I have done so in my own name, attributing the merit to me and not to thee, I have preached Anthony and not Christ, my things and not thy things; therefore I took nothing, except perhaps some croaking frog, certainly not a fish, but a frog that croaked my praises – truly, I took nothing.

A Prayer to Our Lady

We beg you, Our Lady and our hope, you who are Star
  of the Sea,
Illumine your children, engulfed in the turbulent sea of
  sin;
Guide us to the safe harbour of forgiveness,
So we may successfully complete the journey of our
  life
With your protection. With His help
Whom you carried in your womb
And nourished at your holy breasts:
To Him be honour and glory throughout all ages.
    Amen.

A Christmas prayer to Our Lady

Our Lady, the Holy Mother of God, on this day when thy Son was born, who was conceived by thee a virgin, and whom thou hast wrapped in swaddling clothes and rocked in a cradle, intercede on our behalf. Extinguish the flame that the fiery passion of vice has lit up in our souls by thy divine compassion, so that we may finally attain to the joy of heavenly life. May we be granted this grace by Him who deigned to be born of the Virgin: to Him be all honour and glory, for ever and ever. Amen.

A prayer for charity

Lord Jesus,
Bind us to you and our neighbour with love;
May our hearts not be turned away from you,
May our souls not be deceived
Nor our talents and minds enticed
By the allurements of sin,
So that we may never distance ourselves from your
    love.
Thus may we love our neighbour as ourselves,
With strength, wisdom and gentleness,
With your help, you who are blessed
Throughout all the ages.
    Amen.

St Anthony's brief

In the late Thirteenth Century, during the reign of King
Denys of Portugal, lived a woman and her husband in the
town of Santarem. She was troubled by voices, one of
which claimed to be that of Christ, calling on her to drown
herself in the Tagus. Her neighbours considered her sinful,
and her husband had dismissed her as possessed, but she
merely showed signs of schizophrenic behaviour. On her
way to the river she passed a church of the Friars Minor
and went in to pray to St Anthony, to whom she had a
devotion. She asked him pathetically whether he would tell
her if the voices were diabolical or came from God. Then
she fell asleep with exhaustion and had a dream that St
Anthony presented her with a parchment with the words of
his Brief. When she woke, it was lying on her neck, and the
voices ceased to trouble her as long as she kept it. The
words were as follows:

'Behold the cross of the Lord! Begone, you evil powers!
The Lion of the tribe of Judah, the root of David, has
conquered! Alleluia!'

Her husband seems to have been a man of consequence, because he told King Denys the story. The King, who was something of a poet and a musician, and founded the University of Coimbra in 1290, had both learning and imagination, and he was delighted when the husband offered him the parchment. Immediately it left the wife's possession she became disturbed again, but with the help of the Friars Minor her husband obtained a copy from the King and this was just as effective as the original document. The wife made a confession, and lived a holy life for twenty years, ending her days in peace. King Denys kept the brief among his relics; over the centuries, many copies were made, and the words, written on pieces of linen, were regarded almost superstitiously as talismans against evil.

From the 'Sermones Mariales'

This is an extract from a sermon preached by the Saint on the Feast of the Assumption. There was a legend that Our Lady appeared to him on the vigil of the Feast, which was also his birthday.

'On the Bodily Assumption of Mary Into Heaven.'

'And I will glorify the resting place of my feet.'
(Isaiah 60:13)

The resting place of the Lord's feet was Blessed Mary, from whom Christ received His humanity, and who on this day Christ has glorified, by exalting her above the choirs of Angels. Since the resting place of the Lord's feet was the body of the Blessed Virgin, it is clear that she was assumed bodily into Heaven. Hence is it written in the Psalms (131:8) *'Go up, Lord, to your resting place, you and your ark of power.'*
Our Lord went up when he ascended to the Right Hand

of the Father; and the ark of the Lord's power (Mary) went up in that day when she was assumed into the bridal-chamber of heaven. Hence also is it written in Genesis (8:4) that Noah's ark came to rest *'on the mountains of Ararat';* this phrase refers to the angels: the word Ararat means something which has been plucked away, and so those angels who remained steadfast are signified by mountains, and those who fell away by the word Ararat. So you see that Noah's ark is a figure of Mary, through whom we have been given rest from our labours in the land which the Lord has cursed, and today this ark has come to rest on the mountains of Ararat, that is, above the choirs of angels. Expounding this text, we give praise to this same Virgin, who is the Hope of Israel (that is, of Christian people) and add beauty to such a festival...

Today Mary, like another glorious Esther, is led by the hands of angels *'into the chamber of king Ahasuerus'* (Esther 2:15-17), that is, into the heavenly bridal-chamber, where Jesus Christ, the King of Kings, sits on his starry throne. He has loved this glorious Virgin, from whom he took flesh, above all other women, and more than any woman she has found grace and mercy in His presence. O the inestimable dignity of Mary! O indescribable exaltation of grace! O measureless profundity of mercy! When God the Father chose Mary to be the mother of His co-equal Son, begotten before time began, He bestowed on her a grace and dignity greater than had ever been shown to angels or mankind. For a poor woman to be the mother of an emperor's child bestows on her the highest dignity and grace. But the dignity bestowed on Blessed Mary when she became the Mother of God was supremely preeminent. On this day, therefore, she deserved to be crowned, and that is why it says in the same passage in Esther that *'he set the royal diadem on her head.'* In the Song of Songs (3:11) we find the verse: *'Daughters of Sion, come and see King Solomon wearing the diadem with which his mother crowned him on his wedding day',* that is, the day of our Lord's conception, when the divine and human natures, like a bridegroom and

151

bride, were married in the heavenly bridal-chamber of the Virgin. So it is that this same Son has today crowned his Mother with a heavenly diadem. *'Come, therefore, and see the mother of Solomon in the diadem with which her Son has crowned her'* on the day of her assumption!

The day of her assumption was Mary's finest flowering, when she blossomed with joy in the blessedness of celestial glory. Sharing in this great joy, we sing in the Introit of today's Mass: *'Jesus entered a certain village'* (Luke 10:38). The word village, which means a fortified place *(castellum* or *castum)* reminds us of the word chaste *(castus)* and rightly so, since it is chastity which, like a wall round a fortress, prevents the enemy's attacks from breaking through, disturbing our peace and polluting us with fleshly desire. A fortress is surrounded by a wall, and in its midst there is a tower. Mary herself was like a fortress; its walls were her virginity, and its tower her humility. Just as in the Introit the Lord entered the village, so he entered Mary, who was a fortress radiant with the brilliance of complete chastity. The word tower *(turris)* reminds us of the word *'teres'*, meaning something straight and extensive. The humility of Blessed Mary was both of these: straight, because she kept her gaze on Him alone, who had *'looked upon the humility of his handmaid'*; extensive, because through her own humble words: *'Behold the handmaid of the Lord'* (Luke 1:38) Mary was made Queen of Heaven. The Blessed Virgin Mary was both Martha and Mary. Martha, when she wrapped the child in swaddling clothes, laid Him in the manger, fed Him with heavenly milk, fled with Him to Egypt, etc.; Mary, because she *'treasured all these things and pondered them in her heart'* (Luke 2:19).

A responsary of St Anthony

This was written by Julian of Spires, a contemporary of St Anthony. He studied in Paris and lectured there for several years. During the reign of St Louis IX of France he

was choirmaster of the Chapel Royal, and joined the
Franciscan Order late in life. He probably went on the
German mission after the Chapter of 1227, and took his
name from his being stationed at Spires (now Speyer). In
1233 he returned to France, where he both wrote and com-
posed, and died in Paris between 1248-50. His Office of St
Anthony included the lessons from his own Legend of the
Saint, and the Responsary given below. He also wrote an
Office of St Francis, and was only prevented by death from
doing a like service for St Dominic.

If then you ask for miracles,
Death, error, all calamities,
The leprosy and demons fly
And health succeeds infirmities.

The sea obeys and fetters break
And lifeless limbs thou dost restore;
While treasures lost we found again
When young and old thine aid implore.

All dangers vanish at thy prayer
And every need doth quickly flee;
Let those who know thy power tell,
Let Paduans say 'These are of thee.'

The sea obeys and fetters break
And lifeless limbs thou dost restore;
While treasures lost we found again
When young and old thine aid implore.

To Father, Son, may glory be,
And Holy Spirit eternally.

The sea obeys and fetters break
And lifeless limbs thou dost restore;
While treasures lost we found again
When young and old thine aid implore.

Pray for us, blessed Anthony;
that we may be made worthy of the promises of Christ.

O God, may the votive commemoration of Blessed Anthony, your Confessor and Doctor, be a source of joy to your Church, that she may always be fortified with spiritual assistance, and may deserve to possess eternal joy. Through Christ Our Lord. Amen.

Sources

Thomas of Celano was probably the first to mention St Anthony, in the first two books of his life of St Francis. He wrote during Anthony's lifetime.

The Primitive Legend was written at the request of the Minister General of the Order of Friars Minor, between St Anthony's death and his canonisation. It was written by someone who knew St Anthony and had been present at some of the happenings. He also interrogated eye-witnesses, notably Sugerius II, Bishop of Lisbon between 1210 and 1231; several friars and devout citizens gave him their testimonies.

Julian's Legend – part of which formed the Office of St Anthony, and is a contemporary source.

Raimondino's Chronicle was written by a lawyer of Padua who became a Franciscan and heard St Anthony preach from 1227 onward, and has material uniquely his. He died in 1297.

Salimbene of St Adam was only ten when St Anthony died, and so could have seen him. He mentioned St Anthony in his Chronicle of 1231, and tantalisingly said that he would write a complete biography of the Saint, but failed to do so. He joined the Friars Minor in 1238.

Bartholomew of Trent – a Dominican who knew the Saint personally, and wrote an account of his life comparatively early, in 1250.

Dialogus Fratris Crescentii is a collection of episodes in the life of Saints of the Franciscan Order, written at the request of Minister General Crescentius (1244-47). The author was probably John of Parma, who succeeded him as Minister General. The form is the novel one of a dialogue between the Narrator and the Auditor, who elicits information.

The Florentine Legend – found in a legendarium in the Bibliotech Laurentia, in 1902. It seems to date from 1280-1290 and is based on the Julian Legend, but the anonymous Franciscan who wrote it made some embellishments. He was particularly taken by the sermon to the fishes.

The Benignitas Legend – commissioned by Jerome of Ascoli, Minister General of the Franciscan Order, 1274-79, and later Pope Nicholas IV. The author was John of Peckham, later Archbishop of Canterbury, a pupil of St Bonaventure, who may have given him some of the information his account contains. It was approved at the General Chapter of the Order in 1316.

The Legend of Jean Rigaud (sometimes 'Rigauld'). A Friar Minor from Limoges, he became Bishop of Treguier in 1317 and died in 1323; as is to be expected he is expansive in his treatment of the Saint's life in France. He is methodical in his biography, and draws upon many of the earlier sources. The legend was lost for centuries, and only found in the Municipal Library of Bordeaux by Fr Ferdinand Delorme in 1902. A mediaeval scholar left a note in the manuscript, addressed to any possible thief. It assured him that he would be destined for hell fire, and leave black footprints wherever he went in the infernal regions. Fr Rigaud seems to have had access to information not available to other authors. 'Treasures lost are found again' certainly seems to hold true in this case.

Bibliography

Augustine of Hippo and His Monastic Rule. George Lawless, OSA. Clarendon Paperbacks, 1987.

St Anthony of Padua, According to His Contemporaries. E. Gilliat-Smith. J.M. Dent, 1926.

St Anthony of Padua: Doctor of the Church Universal. V. Rev. Raphael Huber. The Bruce Publishing Co. Milwaukee, 1948.

Augustine of Hippo: Selected Writings. Trans. Mary T. Clark. S.P.C.K. London, 1984.

Confessions: St Augustine. Rivingtons, Oxford and London, 1878.

The Catholic Church and History. Hilaire Belloc. Burnes, Oates and Washbourne, 1926.

Saint Anthony of Padua – The Miracle Worker. C.M. Anthony. Longmans, Green and Co, 1911.

St Anthony of Padua. Fr Leopold de Chérancé, trans. Fr Marianus, OSFC. Burnes and Oates, 1895.

The Chronicle of St Anthony of Padua. Ed. Henry James Coleridge, SJ. Burnes and Oates, 1883.

The Augustinians. V. Rev. E.A. Foran, OSA. Burnes, Oates and Washbourne, 1938.

St Anthony and His Times. Mary Purcell. M.H. Gill and Son Ltd., 1960.

Sermons of St Anthony. Antonio Maria Locatelli. Padua, 1895-1903.

The Inquisition. A.L. Maycock. Constable, 1926.

The Great Heresies. Hilaire Belloc. The Catholic Book Club, 1936.

The Primitive Legend of St Anthony of Padua. John Peckham, Archbishop of Canterbury. Washbourne, London, 1897.

Prayers to St Anthony – Praise to You, Lord. Trans. Claude Jarmak. Emp. Edizioni Messaggero, Padua, 1984.

Life of St Anthony (Assidua). Trans. Bernard Przewozny, OFM Conv. Emp. Edizioni Messaggero, Padua, 1984.

St Anthony of Padua, His Life and Teaching. Vergilio Gamboso. Trans. H. Partridge. Emp. Edizioni Messaggero, Padua, 1991.

St Anthony, Doctor of the Church. Sophronius Clasen, OFM. Trans. Ignatius Brady, OFM. Franciscan Herald Press, Chicago, 1961.

The Little Flowers of St Anthony of Padua. Ed. Luigi Guidaldi, OFM Conv. Trans. George D. Smith. Burnes, Oates and Washbourne, 1936.

Saint Dominic. Jean Guiraud. Duckworth and Co. London, 1901.

The Little Flowers of St Francis of Assisi. Trans. T.W. Arnold. Chatto and Windus, 1908.

St Francis of Assisi. G.K. Chesterton. Hodder and Stoughton, 1923.

St Anthony of Padua. Albert Lepitre. R. and T. Washbourne Ltd., 1917.

St Anthony of Padua. Nello Vann. Burnes, Oates and Washbourne, 1936.

Anthony of Padua, Saint, Apostle and Wonderworker. Roger Maloney, OFM. The Antonian Press, Dublin, 1931.

The Moral Concordances of St Anthony of Padua. Rev. J.M. Neale. Ellis and Keene, 1898.

St Francis of Assisi. Thomas of Celano. Trans. Placid Hermann, OFM. Franciscan Herald Press, Chicago, 1963.

Life of St Bonaventure. Trans. L.C. Skey. Burnes and Oates.

A Franciscan View of Life – St Bonaventure. Trans. Dominic Devas, OFM. Thomas Baker, London, 1922.

Seek First His Kingdom – St Anthony of Padua. Ed. Fr Livio Poloniato, OFM. Conv. Conventual Franciscan Friars, 1988.

Popular Religion in the Middle Ages. Rosalind and Christopher Brooke. Thames and Hudson, 1984.

St Francis of Assisi. John Holland Smith. Sidgwick and Jackson, 1972.

Francis of Assisi – A Portrait. E.M. Almedingen. The Bodley Head, 1967.

St Anthony of Padua – Doctor of the Church Universal. Catholic University of America, Washington D.C., 1947.